what she taught me

J.L. FORD

Copyright © 2019 J.L.Ford

All rights reserved. This book or parts thereof may not be reproduced in any form, stored in any retrieval system, or transmitted in any form by any means—electronic, mechanical, photocopy, recording, or otherwise—without prior written permission of the publisher, except as provided by United States of America copyright law. For permission requests, write to the publisher, at "Attention: Permissions Coordinator," at authorjlford@gmail.com

ISBN-13: 978-0-9895965-8-9 – Print
ISBN-10: 0-9895965-8-3

ISBN-13: 978-0-9895965-9-6 Ebook
ISBN-10: 0-9895965-9-1

Contents

Foreword 5

Introduction 10

Chapter 1   The Destroyer and the Distraction 29

Chapter 2   Avoiding Disaster 44

Chapter 3   The Light 61

Chapter 4   What Love Is 79

Chapter 5   The Muse 90

Chapter 6   Connection, Commitment,
and Marriage 108

Chapter 7   The Healer 132

Chapter 8   Intimacy and Loving 154

Next Steps 171

About the Author 173

Foreword

Sylvester McNutt III

A few years ago I knew I wanted to be a full-time motivational speaker after finding success as an author. However, I was unsure of how I was going to do it. I did all I could on my own, but even still, I needed an established professional to share some insider information. The universe guided me to one—J.L. Ford. I was a rookie as a speaker, but J.L. respected me as an author, as a peer, and most importantly as a human. I vividly remember asking J.L. to share some insight on his experience as a motivational speaker. Time and information that I should have been charged a consultation fee for. This story speaks to the kind of man J.L. truly is. He did not ask me to pay him anything. He did not make me feel as if I was wasting his time; in fact, he was welcoming and open. He was eager to share, to teach, and to see another person advance. He provided information openly and never asked for anything in return. I will never forget the kind energy that was bestowed upon me. This gesture showed me something about his heart and character: they are infinite.

As years go by, our friendship grows, and then comes an offer from J.L. that left me—an author—totally speechless.

"Sylvester, I want you to write the foreword in my newest book."

That gesture is a reflection of the compassionate and elaborate tone that J.L. operates with daily. When you read the words in this book, you will experience the exact same feeling of joy, gratitude, happiness, love, and acceptance that I felt when he made his request. It was such a good feeling to read the book and to see those same emotions reflected throughout his writing. I could feel the love and honest place that J.L. speaks and writes from. A lot of the times when people talk about love, they are talking about their idealistic views of it, but here, you see that this perception of love comes from experience.

The words here make you feel the depths of love, the expansion of internal understanding, and pushes your mind to break up with your predetermined notions about love. Each idea mingles together to show the duality between energy, between our own structures, between our own truth. What I love about the book is how J.L. instantly pulls us into a world of introspection, as we begin to clearly see what structures are and how we have built them. When J.L. wrote, "With each person you meet, you experience a new part of yourself," in chapter 3, a deep sense of nirvana came over my soul. Jereme has stories, poems, and realistic thoughts that make the reader feel as if they're floating through a bubble of love. I will visit this book over and over, especially because J.L. has a style that is poetic, yet real and direct. When it comes to love, none of us want to play games or to be sold a bunch of stories that aren't real. Everything is real here.

As a man, I can appreciate his directness and commitment to telling his truth. When my lady reads the book, she will love the imagination and analogies that offer deeper insight. But as a man who loves feminine energy, I also like how he breaks down the duality and connection between our energies—never pitting them against each other, but showing us how we can continue to keep in alignment. Writing to both the feminine and masculine energy, while respecting both and lifting both up, is tough—in this book, J.L. Ford's words do that and much more.

The Oracle

It was the deeper parts of her mind that commanded my attention, intrigued me, inspired me, and played a detrimental role in a sharp pivot in my thinking, and as a result, my life. The Oracle is the wise woman. She is the one who lives among beings and sees through them, who operates within societal structures, well aware most of it is nonsensical yet necessary.

She would speak well beyond my grasp. For a time, I was unable to discern whether she was speaking from a place I had not reached mentally, or if most of her thoughts were simply a bit unhinged. Teetering somewhere in the middle, my curiosity had been piqued to the point of action. In testing her thoughts and ideas, it did not take long to find myself face-to-face with my own ignorance and delusions. Needless to say, the Oracle is not unhinged. She, a truly enlightened being, is the one who set me on the adventure of spiritual and mental growth that made this book and my new life possible. For that, I will always owe her a debt of gratitude.

Introduction

When it comes to evolving, there is no such thing as an arrival, nor a finish line. It simply keeps going. As you progress through phases, you see less people and the air gets a little thinner, but it keeps going. The lessons do not become any easier. Just when you think you have it all down, that you have come to a place where you can rest, you find the end of one progression and the beginning of another. A whole new journey, if you will. As daunting as this may seem, it is the course that we set out for ourselves the moment we first asked the question: "Who am I?" There is no real answer, as we are ever evolving; however, every now and again we get a chance to feel like the cat who caught its tail, if only for a moment. There is no arrival, only a place where one may pitch his tent and settle. That, too, will be the place where he stops growing.

But even then, the pitch is never quite safe from unsuspecting winds and our own curiosity.

This book is the product of a major progression in my life. One that started on a beach with four wise women who, at that time, were little more than strangers. What I thought would be an hour or so of enjoying the water and sunset with beautiful women, turned into a night of them teaching as I listened intently. The women, who I refer to as the Coven, allowed me access to their world in a way that women are rarely able to give men, even if they desire to or try. Those lessons set off a chain of events that would include the destruction of things I did and did not care for, yet were significant in my life. I also found myself open to experiences and lessons that I otherwise would have never given myself the chance to know.

By the end of it all, I found myself as a new man. A man that I did not know could exist. The road there was difficult, sometimes even devastating, but I had been offered a new life in line with my higher self, and I accepted.

As much paradise as I saw around me, I could not help but notice the lack of other men enjoying the same, and so, I began a new journey. One with a finish line and a potentially life-altering point for you.

I will admit that as much as I have felt compelled to, I've always been wary about writing books geared toward men. This is because men are an overwhelming minority when it comes to who is picking up books, and every reader wants their words read. But what I have learned during this journey is how much change can happen in the world when one person changes, and even if the eyes of only a few men see the inside of this book, it will be worth the labor.

This book is my story and includes many of the lessons I have picked up throughout my latest progression. This book is my gift to you. I do not consider myself to be greater than any man. We all walk on the same road, just at different points. This book is you and I coming to a point on your path. It is my sincerest hope you find a treasure within these pages. Something that, when all is said and done, adds a sweetness to your life that you may otherwise have never savored.

Namaste.

The Destroyer

Her beauty was easily the most captivating of any woman I had ever seen walk the earth. The feminine energy she possessed was so powerful, alluring, and intoxicating. She was the magnetic force that effortlessly willed me in its direction, by merely existing, as I destroyed everything that stood between the two of us along that path.

Construction and destruction are the equally necessary functions of divine feminine energy, the moving entity of the ever-creating source. She embodied the destructive force, the part of creation that revels in the beauty of things that cost far more than they're worth. She meant no harm, however harm must exist in order to make space for the birth of things beautiful and new. She was the serpent who asked "what if?" when the question alone was taboo, and the God who promised to cleanse the world with fire to make way for a perfect home. She was the bewitching distraction that I could not turn my eyes away from, which was as it was meant to be. In order for any Destroyer to play its part in one's life, it must be undeniably attractive to that person. Her presence alone made me forget every responsibility that I had, momentarily forcing me into the peace of simply being. It was as though she was designed specifically for me during that time, so that much of what I had built could be tragically brought to dust, debris, and rubble, which allowed for me to begin carving the foundation for something new.

The Distraction

The Distraction was a youthful beauty, wise beyond her time, yet harboring a swell of pain that could easily turn her into a potent Destroyer. Destroyers often begin as Distractions. It is the phase where they learn how easily they can capture the attention of others. At times, they find it astounding, even exhilarating, what people are willing to move their energy away from just to pay attention to them. Eyes are taken off families, marriages, careers, finances, and health just to catch a glimpse of the Distraction, and many have fallen as a result.

Her place is not without purpose. She is to that which we hold dear as the rustling wind is to a tree. Her presence alone tests how focused one is on what is valued, or if it is actually valued at all. With gratitude and acknowledgment of her, her role can be used for one's gain. However, ignoring the fact that the Distraction has usurped your attention could be the beginning of a catastrophe.

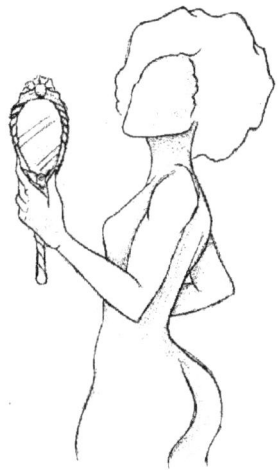

The Muse

It was the way she walked that caught my attention. Her posture was statuesque and imposing, yet she moved gracefully with her head held as high as the clouds. There was so much length in her stride, every movement of every part of her body was powered with a glowing feminine energy of purpose. Her presence was regal and felt by everyone her energy touched. She was a moving river of confidence, encapsulated in a body that many would be surprised by. After all, her skin leaned to the darker chocolate, her youth was reminiscent of a blooming rose, she looked up to most in standing conversation, and perhaps most importantly, she was a woman.

I knew nothing of her, but I knew that I wanted her near me. I would later learn that indeed I needed her, at least for a while.

I needed her because in all of her grace and giving of love, she could see right through my persona and had no trouble savagely tearing apart my ego. She is the personified force who steadied my view in the mirror and forced me to see the deepest parts of myself.

She was the storm of intelligence that few would see coming. Stirred by her truths yet steadied with gratitude. As much as I could be, I was quiet in her presence. She is a woman, who since antiquity, has inspired men to look within. Never to be forgotten, she is the Muse.

The Light

The Light was what we all come into this world as, a pure part of the story that feels magical despite how hard other areas of life may be. People were drawn to her just as they are drawn to a newborn, just as they are drawn to the sun. The warmth of both rescues them, it causes them to forget their fears and hardships, if only for a moment. Ironically, it is what they love about her that causes envy to stir within them. That envy thrives because they wonder, when it comes to suffering, why me and not her? Because they cannot see that she has her pain too, and because they cannot see that without her existence there would be nothing more in the world than what we spend most days praying to be relieved of—darkness.

All lights dim in their own time, and it is more common than not that this world will cause that to happen prematurely. I saw the Light's relevance to darkness, and to sickness, which is why I took it upon myself to protect her from all conceivable threats to her innocence. I wanted darkness and sickness to have her, without turning her into what they are.

They come with empty hands, they come with the suffering that we must all endure, and most of all they come with the greatest threat of all—reality. They come to take away her light so they do not have to suffer in misery alone.

Protecting the mesmerizing water globe in which she lived was a crushing burden that I happily imposed on myself, one that became the catalyst for the greatest lessons of my life.

The Feminine

Her eyes were the first thing about her to catch my attention. They were big, a deep emerald green, and piercing. Time may well rob me of the memory of how she looks otherwise, but I will never forget her eyes. I explored them with curiosity; there was an overwhelming feeling that I had seen them before. Maybe it was a different lifetime, should such a thing exist, or maybe it was a subtle sign that our crossing paths was a significant event that was meant to be.

I learned the most from her about myself and feminine energy by being still and witnessing her be. I listened to her sing the sweetest notes and dance as though she were performing in front of an audience gazing in awed silence. I watched her sit in the sand and create waves with the sea. Her energy was exhilarating and magnetic, and her touch was gentle while replete with love and healing power.

As I stood in my own masculine energy, I found myself enamored with her feminine energy, as has always been the case between the two. The feminine, unlike its counterpart, is constant motion. It is colorful, expressive, creative, and unencumbered. To the masculine, the feminine is a radiant and beautiful force of chaos that he cannot be close enough to, and yet farther away from.

The Logician

The Logician played the role of translator for many of the lessons that were relayed to me while watching the Coven. She was able to do this because while physically she is a woman, her energy is strongly masculine. This allowed her to experience both the masculine and the feminine and serve as a translator to either side.

Unlike femininity, masculinity is structured and logical. It is very this or that, black or white. And unlike the movement of femininity, it represents stillness like that of a mature sequoia tree. Still, the two need each other to survive. After all, what would a beautiful home be without a frame? Or a symphony without musical notes? While the movement of the feminine is chaotic to the masculine, it is only because of its nature as the exact opposite, and it is for that same reason that the masculine is so attracted to the feminine.

One of the most important things that the Logician was able to show me was my ignorance of the feminine. It truly was a revelation as to the level of cluelessness that I, and most men, have as it related to her energy as well as our own. In one lesson alone, she opened a door to the feminine that most will never see, and because of her insight and willingness to teach me, I can open that door and potentially many others for you.

The Healer

The Healer is in tune with the energy of the earth and all souls like no other. She finds joy in the life of all, but aches from the cloud of misery that blankets this world. She sees through the eyes and to the deepest parts of hearts and is more than willing to take on the pain of another just so that less of it can exist in the world. However, in most instances, there is no need.

Her words, her eyes, and her energy are all healing. Her touch as well, can repair the deepest wounds. She is the broken soul that mends hearts. She is the Healer.

In order for the masculine to surrender his pain to her, she makes herself extremely vulnerable. Her touch demolishes the walls that many believed were impenetrable. Her eyes follow his, cutting through to the deepest parts of him. Mentally she is a step ahead, always countering his silence with patience, and his defenses with wit. She allows herself to be poured into, and he accepts her offer because he knows that she is strong, fearless, resilient, and most of all, she will not judge him.

The Whole Woman

Sometimes I think I should retire from attempting to describe her. It has proven to be an impossible feat. However, I will never give up, because in the moment where I am searching for the words, I feel her so intensely. She is the most amazing being. An ocean of loving energy created from the far-reaching spectrum of bliss and pain. She has walked through the most noxious fires and has been cooled by healing rains. She moves throughout this world with mesmerizing grace and an unapologetic strength. Her arms are always extended, giving love to anything she feels with a touch as soft as downy feathers. The first time we embraced, it felt as though she was holding the ailing child inside of me, and it was there, wrapped in her healing arms, that I instantly fell in love. She is what every man needs but most men are afraid of. The destroyer and the builder. The fighter and the lover. The entire sun and the darkness that it illuminates. A liberated work of pulchritudinous art that may only be bound by love. She is the Whole Woman whose presence alone is a lesson of love for all who desire to know.

Chapter 1

The Destroyer and the Distraction

The Destroyer came into my life as a Distraction, and by the time she walked away, my marriage with the Light had been devastated. The Distraction had usurped my attention and become the Destroyer, and before I knew it, I was left standing in the rubble of my structure's ruins. Imagine, standing in a structure you placed so much energy into building, and even more into maintaining, only to find yourself surrounded by the charred embers of its fragmented remains. Most likely you do not have to imagine this scenario to understand what it feels and looks like, because most likely you have stood amongst your own fallen structures before. Perhaps at this very moment you are standing before debris from a structure you built. It is so often the unfortunate story of many men, to time and time again build structures, short and tall, only to be buried under them after the structure's untimely demise. And so, this is where we will build the foundation of this book—at the very beginning in which we attempt to understand what we are building, why we continue to build, why we create in a way that attracts destruction, and what we can do to avoid unnecessary suffering.

Structures

Just as the spider weaves his web, we all build structures. Structures are the relationships that we have with the people in our lives, what we do for work and how we go about it, the organizations that we are a part of, our social media accounts and how we manage them, our homes and the way we organize them, how we choose to govern ourselves while wearing our array of masks for various occasions, and how we manage to exist within a community.

Take a moment to think about your personal structures, which I will refer to as micro-structures. These structures are the ways in which you have chosen to build your life. When you peer into them, you see the endless structures inside of each one, examples of this include your house rules in your home structure, your routine in your personal business structure, and the core values of your personality structure. Now, if you stand outside of these micro-structures, you will find that the structures *you* are operating in are not even your own. These I refer to as macro-structures—think culture, language, politics, nationality, beliefs, and the entire system of patriarchy. While they can be affected by you (in most cases only minimally), their creation predates you in most cases, and they are constantly being molded independently of you.

We all weave our own micro-structures, the webs that are personal and individualized, but one of the greatest privileges of being a man in this society is that men are the creators of the macro-structures. This means that the overarching structures in which we all exist are, for the most part, created for the benefit of men and the masculine essence. No matter the macro-structure, be it religion, government, business, or in the home, it is much more likely than not that a man will be found at the top, weaving the web that others must learn how to survive in.

The Curse of Attraction

As we move throughout these discussions of the masculine and feminine, keep in mind that neither are assigned to bodies, genders, or sex. We are all duel-natured beings holding the essence of both the masculine and the feminine. However, we all have our place on the spectrum between the two. As a man, your masculine essence is likely to be dominant, whereas the essence of a woman is likely to be feminine. To reiterate, this does not have to be the case, as women can be predominantly masculine and men predominantly feminine. The key is to understand the difference between the two, recognizing the energy that is opposite of your dominant energy, and having gratitude for it all. This is the way to balance and intimacy, whereas suppressing one leads to toxicity in your relationship with self and others. Although the masculine and feminine continue to push across boundaries of gender and sexuality, for the purposes of this book, our exploration will generally be exemplified as men embodying masculine energy (with the exception of the Logician) and women embodying feminine energy. These are concepts that we will explore more deeply as we move throughout this book.

One threat that our micro-structures face it that of attraction, which I define as the pull of the masculine and feminine to become one again. It is as much as a solution as it is a problem, as it can be, and often becomes, a catalyst for destruction when there is a lack of respect and appreciation for the function of both the masculine and the feminine as well as the process of the two becoming one.

I began with the topic of structures because it is the nature of your masculine energy to build, understand, and find comfort in structures. However, what this energy is attracted to is its polar opposite. In other words, though masculine nature is stillness, you will always be drawn to the free and moving nature of the feminine. This attraction by the masculine energy exists while simultaneously judging the feminine as untrustworthy, chaotic, and reckless because it opposes the masculine essence. Therefore, while the masculine may delight in the dance with the feminine, if your masculine energy is not understanding and grateful for the divine nature of the feminine, you will inevitably attempt to change feminine energy to something more tolerable and comfortable. Something that you understand. Something masculine.

You love her sexuality but you shame it, you love the sway of her hips and the way her clothes hug them, but you want her to be more conservative so as not to draw attention, you love her free and intellectual thinking, but you always want her to be your student. This happens quite often and in many ways, as men kill what they love about their feminine partners in order to feel secure. For the sake of love and sometimes security, many women will find themselves allowing their feminine energy to be stifled, and what they receive in return is their feminine energy-deprived partner looking for that same divine feminine energy outside of the relationship. In something they are not tethered to, someone who cannot break their fragile egos and hearts.

Then there is the feminine, who, while attracted to

the still nature of the masculine, finds it inconceivable for herself to exist in such a way. What she is attracted to is the safety of that stillness, which allows her to flourish in her femininity. She can exist within and outside of the structure, but being the structure would effectively kill her, as she then would become masculine. She sees the safety, but she also sees a danger in it, therefore she invites the masculine to dance freely. She's not trying to change him, she is trying to love him. She wants him to feel the joy and relief of letting go. She wants him to surrender his mind, his body, his emotions, and his feelings, but not too much, because then she shames him for doing the very thing she asked for. Just as the feminine cannot be still too long, the masculine cannot dance for long, as he then will lose himself to the feminine. When that happens, she will leave him and find masculinity elsewhere.

The attraction between the two will always be, as all of attraction is, simply the desire for the masculine and feminine to be one again. The potential for threats to micro- and macro-structures can be found in the actions we take to become closer to our polar opposite as we submit to attraction. As we connect with our partners we tend to either change so they may feel safe, or demand them to change for our own sense of safety. This occurs as we understand what safety means to our partners as well as to ourselves. While there are some ideals, values, and expectations that are solidified as safe, there will always be moving parts and changes as to what safety means as we change and relate to new people. In my past, I may have considered a woman who did not swear as some form of safety. This is a woman I would consider of virtue, as I had been raised to think. Today, I tend to trust more the people who passively express themselves with profanity. There's a realness to it that allows me to be a little more comfortable around them. It is a seemingly small example, but not so much when you consider how many potentially good partners you cannot connect with because of small judgments over something as the type of words they choose to use. As it relates to the masculine and feminine, safety is found in stillness just as freedom is found in movement. The masculine will attempt to rein the feminine in because he sees the lack of safety in her dance, for her as well as himself. Indeed, a part of the controlling nature of a man can be attributed to the fact that he genuinely cares. However, as we will discuss in chapter 5, his concern is not needed as much as he thinks and his actions that follow those concerns can become toxic. The feminine who has balance with the masculine understands the safety in masculine, and if she does not, she learns as soon as trouble brews, as we all run back to our sound structure when roaring thunder breaks through the sky and shakes the foundation of the earth.

There is a natural order to connecting; however, because of our fears, ideals, values, and desires, it is all too often achieved by force. How we force others to change and how we are forced to change can cause injury on the individual level and create toxicity on micro and macro levels, simply because we cannot appreciate our polar opposite, and allow what we love and desire to simply be. For example, men are often considered weak by all genders just for displaying emotions; similarly, a boundary of shame and guilt has been built around many women to capsulate their sexuality or overall feminine expression. On a larger scale, it can be seen in the crushing pressure placed on men who are reduced to a sole role of providing, and the long-standing act of oppressing feminine voices that dare to demand change from the patriarchal norm.

There has to be balance, meaning, the feminine has to be the feminine, the masculine has to be the masculine, and both have to embrace the bit of each other that resides within. Anything else causes imbalance and ultimately separation. The Light is a victim of imbalance, as she had been raised in a religion where there is little room for femininity, and it is only femininity in a very specific and rigid way. Her father's place in the family is unquestionably at the head, and his masculinity is so toxic that it affects all who live within or dependent on his structure. His actions and beliefs show that he considers the suppression of the feminine as a form of love through protection, but from what I have witnessed in all the women in his life, his ways are nothing more than violence against an essential part of themselves. This injury to the Light also created a sizable void in our relationship. The energy that I grew to so desperately need was the same energy that her father had stifled, and it was the one thing the Destroyer had that could usurp my attention away from the structure I had placed so much effort into creating.

You and your structures

For so long I wondered why men would build such astonishing structures just to make one move that would cause their utter destruction. In my first book, I wrote of a mentor who, despite have an amazing family, would routinely risk everything by sleeping with women he had little to no actual care for. That's common among the general population of men, but then there are the mega pastors, world leaders, and successful businessmen who do the same. They spend their best years weaving something remarkable, and then they allow themselves to be distracted just long enough to see the whole thing go up in smoke, with everyone in it having to suffer as well.

You will create your structure, you will then either stand inside of the structure, sit outside of it, or a combination of the two. One who stands inside of his structure takes the structure very seriously. The maintenance and security of his structure is of utmost importance to him. This can ultimately be crushing to him, and toxic as well. On the other hand, the man who exists outside of the structure he builds cares little for structure. He created it for whatever reason and is not concerned with what happens to it. The man who builds his structures and spends time both in and out of it sees the structure as valuable, be that value for those inside of it, or for what can be personally gained from it. He sees the value in not being inside of it at all times or taking it too seriously. In any case, it is inevitable that we build, and it would be wise that we do it with the weaknesses of the structure in mind.

Despite how disastrous our carelessness always proves itself to be, men continue to build structures with glaring weaknesses that will leave the structure to call for the Destroyer to do her work. There are many reasons for this, including: societal and cultural pressures, trying to prove something to oneself or, for many men, prove something to their fathers; also sometimes we build faulty structures because we care too much about the opinions of the people who need or are strongly attached to the structures. Such as taking up a career that makes our parents happy, or saying "I do" because marriage is the demand of the person we wish to spend our life with.

It is foolish, not because any of it matters, but because the people who depend on the structures matter to the builders of them. These people, who may be anything from an acquaintance to a loved one, care deeply for the structure built for them and in many cases rely on it for their survival. Every day, employees go to work with an expectation of security within their workplace structure, your family and loved ones look for the same in the structures they have with you. People depend on you to build and maintain your structure with foresight, wisdom, and care. If ever you find yourself standing in the rubble of a structure that should have survived much longer, you will wish that you had taken more care as well.

You should also care because you are standing under that same structure, and you cannot escape the trouble that comes from it falling onto you as well. You will find yourself straining under the weight of a structure that you don't give enough of a fuck about. Sure, you may care about it, but not enough to keep your eyes away from the distractions that threaten it. You will find yourself holding your structure, still struggling, stressed, and exhausted, and then out of the corner of your eye you will notice a free spirit moving about. It will say: "Come with me, be free." Be it small or large, it will be enough to take your attention away from your structure, which is all that it takes for the whole thing to come down. Perhaps the distraction is a dream of a different life, maybe it's a job, but we know that more often than not, it will be another woman. One you would be too terrified to build a structure with but would delight in the escape that she promises. Whatever it might be, it would not be much of a distraction at all if you were holding onto a structure that truly matters to you.

How the feminine suffers

A quick note on the feminine. Know that she suffers similarly, however it differs from the masculine in that when her pouring into structures is freely done, it is motivated by love rather than necessity or duty. I am reminded of my mother, who has given so much of herself to her marriage, her children, her church, and her job. She has been consistent in this since I have known her. I could always see that she gave more than most because she was *being* from her heart. This is a part of what makes the feminine invaluable for the health of any given structure. It is also the reason why the feminine is so often taken for granted. Because their heart is in their actions, they will do more for less—less money, less praise, less status, less respect, and less appreciation. People who will do more for less are often less compensated. While this is not reasonable, it is in a sense rational. Why give what is due to someone who will accept less? Clearly the answer is, "because what is due is deserved." It is also clear that many in a position of power are too greedy to fairly compensate. For the feminine, what she lacks in compensation may be made up in the reward she feels in the results of her labor. Still, just as is the case for the masculine, these rewards have their limits.

All of this to say, be wary of a man buried under the weight of heavy structures to which he actually cares too little for, as well as the woman who cares for the structure she shares but receives very little in return from those who benefit from her. Neither of them are in a healthy balance with their structures, and it ultimately could cost them much, if not everything.

A part of the aftermath of my marital structure being destroyed was the almost immediate departure of the Light. I could not blame her, for as much as I needed the rush of free-flowing feminine energy, I could feel that she needed the surrendering intimacy of the masculine. She was attached to the structure, and she loved it. The only thing that she wanted more than the structure to survive, was for me to care about the structure in the way that she did, and for me to look at her the way I looked at what distracted me from it. I cared little for the structure. I cared a great deal for the Light. I care about my own well-being, but I did not care enough to muster up the courage to do something about fixing my structure before life, time, opportunity, and the Destroyer took care of it for me.

Chapter 2

Avoiding Disaster

The structure of my marriage was a methodical build, and one that started long before paths of the Light and I ever crossed. The foundation of this structure was made of adopted beliefs as to what a marriage, a wife, and a husband should be. Its framework mirrored the same. At a time when I felt I had become what a husband should be, I set out to find the perfect wife to fit in this structure, and when I did, I pulled out all stops to move her into it. I sold or gave away most of my belongings, uprooting myself from a paradise I said I would never leave, moved to what is easily the most miserable area of North America, then spent the next few years fighting for the heart of the Light, and the approval of her father, who merely tolerated me, despite all of my efforts. Eventually I won the man over, enough so that he would officiate the wedding, but as I will explain further, it was on that wedding day, standing in front of her and before him, that I realized I was building a structure almost certain to fail.

This is not a unique story. Many have stood at the altar, imagining saving themselves by bolting to the door, only to choke out a painful "I do" through a seemingly genuine smile. There's a lot of pressure to deliver that "I do" in the moment, and even knowing we should not, we do it anyway, before turning around to face the barrel of the rest of our lives while everyone in the congregation cheers us on. For me, it was not about love, as my love for the Light was something I was sure of. The problem was that I had realized the foundation of my structure was fatally flawed, which will always make the entire structure weak, no matter how well it is constructed. This is a lesson that I had to learn the incredibly hard way. I went through with the wedding because I did not want to let the Light down in that moment, and I had convinced myself that if I just work hard enough on the structure, it would overcome the weakness of the foundation. I was wrong.

At the time I was not entirely sure of what I was missing, but I did know that missing piece was also the weakest point of my marriage, and by the time I did find it, the Destroyer had already identified it and was making her way toward it like a wrecking ball traveling at a blazing speed. When she connected, the entire structure came crashing down. Even while I was entrenched in rubble and misery, I held no resentment toward her, not even as she walked away. I knew that she was simply playing her part in my story, and I was grateful that the destruction happened when it did, so I may have a chance to build from the unflappable foundation of truth.

Because of its weak foundation, my marital structure with the Light was destined for destruction. As much as we resisted it, it had to be this way. The collapse or utter destruction of a structure is often necessary, and at times inevitable. Any structure that has been destroyed either had its weak points ignored or its builder and sustainer attracted what led to the structure's ultimate demise. In other words, the Destroyer is essentially compelled by your highest self to annihilate anything that does not serve your best interests. In my situation it was both. Not only had I ignored the weak points of the structure, but my strain to keep it together had become a beckoning call for help, a rescue from something that I refused to destroy myself. While I could have reduced the amount of carnage by practicing self-love and tearing down my structure with careful intention, by leaving my fate in the hands of hope and self-sabotage, I ultimately chose a path that led to disaster.

With every structure that you build, you should know there may come a day when it will need serious attention, or the whole thing might come down. A structure without weak points will not be destroyed. A structure with a nourished and strong foundation will not be destroyed. A structure that is truly valued will not be destroyed. Strong and valued structures that do fall, do not go down without a fight, and the odds are strongly in favor of those structures being built once again, stronger than before. But not all structures are strong, and a man must work intentionally to ensure a sound structure.

In terms of acting on his structures with intent, a man recognizes the fault lines of his structures and acts in his own best interest, whether that entails carefully destroying the structure in a way that causes the least harm to himself and others, or simply working to repair those fault lines to sustain the structure. In the opposite scenario, he ignores the fault lines of his structure, as well as the immense pressure of holding it all together. In such a scenario, the highest self will always prevail on the behalf of the individual, as hell is living in contrary to one's true self. Be it consciously or subconsciously, constructively or destructively, we will always attempt to rescue ourselves from hell. With a weak structure that's doomed to fall, the important part is choosing the path of rescue that will do the least amount of harm.

To put it plainly, you want to avoid as much unnecessary destruction as possible. The following suggestions are not pieces of advice that will allow one to avoid destruction all together, as destruction is an inevitable and necessary factor in creation. Rather the advice relates to approaching destruction with intent as opposed to allowing it to simply happen to you. We are the architects of much of our reality, and with that, there is the responsibility to utilize destruction in our favor. When we lose sight of or outright ignore the responsibility of carefully and thoughtfully dismantling structures that are not serving our highest self, life happens to us, opening the door for destruction to befall us in surprising, and at times excruciating ways.

Take the time to understand, as much as possible, the structures that you have thoughtlessly adopted and have adapted to over the span of your lifetime. We all do it, as adopting and adapting to structures is a matter of survival. This is why your parents began the process of teaching and indoctrinating you moments after you were born. You must explore each structure that you are attached to in order find what truly benefits you, your purpose, and how you wish to exist during this brief experience of life. Accomplishing these feats will prove nearly impossible while operating within the structure with which you are focused. As difficult as it can be, you will find it much more beneficial to step out of the structure to see it all. During this exercise, you must be mindful that many of the structures that predate your existence have safeguards to prevent you from stepping out for even a moment, such as a religion's threat of eternal punishment at the blink of an eye or the shaming that one would experience from doing something as unheard of as taking a break from their marriage. Other consequences may not be as damning. However, in many situations, all it will take for those close to you to turn away is for you to pause acting within the societal and cultural norms. While existing and operating inside of a structure you may truly believe in, it can be difficult to see how harmful it is to you. There are many people in abusive relationships right now who have no clue as to how much they are being broken down daily, and they may not realize it until they have become completely broken.

Once you truly see the structure and what it means for your experience, you must be willing to accept the truth of the entire matter. Often we fail to do this because with truth comes responsibility. Once you realize the weakness of your structure, or that something is not working in your favor, it is an act of betrayal and even violence against yourself to do nothing about it, because to do nothing is to allow more harm to come to you. Consider some of the bombs that went off in your own life as it relates to structures in the past; you most likely did not see them coming because you believed in your structure. The question you must ask yourself is: Did I believe in this structure on my own accord, or did I accept as true something that someone else believed in? While the structure may have benefited that individual or most of society, it does not mean the same will be true for you. There are many men and women who delight in the benefits of patriarchy, while many fight the oppressive nature of it, just as there are many children who suffer in the religious structures that their parents have thrived in.

You must question every structure that you were given to ensure that it is in sync with your truest self. If it is not, you must either restructure it in a way that does or abandon it altogether.

Examine all the structures that you have placed yourself inside of. You can find these structures in your daily routines; pay attention to your thoughts, actions, and even where you transport your body as well as the length of time you keep it there. This may sound odd, but the purpose of your body is to be your vehicle to experience yourself in this world. How much of that can you do while hunched over, typing on a computer in a cubicle for eight hours a day? Most people spend much of their days in a place they do not wish to be, leading them to thoughts of wishing their weeks away for the weekend. Ask yourself if you are truly happy with where you sleep and who you are sleeping with, if you enjoy where you live, if a short commute in your car is really worth the payments you are making for it, if your status among others is worth the personal cost to you, if your friends are filling or draining you, if your eating habits are an act of love for your body or if you are slowly destroying it, if you treat people the way you would like to be treated, and if your spending habits are supporting your financial goals. In every single moment, you are acting or existing within some structure, and you are completely responsible for ensuring that it adds to your overall health and experience of life rather than taking from them.

You must care for your structure as much as you care for those who benefit from it. This is especially true if your contribution to the structure is what keeps it afloat. As briefly discussed previously, you can easily find yourself living in, creating, or sustaining a structure for someone else, whether you care for the structure itself or not.

On one occasion the Light told me about a man who often comes to her for advice on food and health. She shared that the man was very out of shape and suffered many physical ailments. When asked what he felt was the cause of his decline in health, the man shared that his job as a lawyer is extremely stressful, but he has stayed in the profession to provide a good life for his daughters and wife. These are noble ambitions, but the price he is paying mentally and physically while his family lives an amazing and healthy life is in fact an act of violence against himself. He is not alone. Many men hold on to burdening structures for others and for many reasons. If they had the chance to let it go without seeing their loved ones suffer as a result, they would toss it without hesitation. One must look to what will become of it all at some point if the structure is not reconstructed or destroyed right away. Any problem that you do not deal with today will more than likely evolve into an emergency. Structures crashing are often emergencies. When a structure crashes to the ground, those who benefit from it go down with it. This often is a cause of resentment, which itself is a silent killer of relationships.

The antidote is always the same: restructure or destroy. In the lawyer's case, imagine the difference in the quality of life he would experience should he elect to give up practicing, or at the very least decide to practice law in a way that does not tax him as much. Sure, his family may see a decline in extravagance, but I would surmise that the extra quality time they will receive with a healthy father would matter a great deal more. Of course, this is easier said than done, especially when the costs of pulling away from a structure are much higher, such as the structure of marriage or faith. The costs can be emotional, cultural, familial, financial, and so on. You just must ask yourself how much your happiness is worth to you. Living your life for the benefit of others in a way that drains you is the quickest way to death. I am not referring simply to physical death, as for some, that would be relief. I am referring to the emotional and mental death en route to that end.

Ensure that you are continuously poured into as you continuously pour into the structures that you love. We love to give to people and structures in ways that make us feel alive inside, but giving requires that there is something within to give. This is a lesson that I remember learning as a very young child, when after saving my money for a year, I gave it all away while on the way to buy food at a local restaurant. I was in Atlanta, Georgia, at the time for our annual church convention, which was something we looked forward to as much as most kids look forward to Christmas. I had worked in the painstakingly hot fields of Florida throughout the year to ensure that I could really enjoy our brief stay in the city. One morning I decided to have a breakfast at the most amazing place a child could, McDonald's. As I happily walked down the few blocks leading to the golden-arched palace, I encountered several panhandlers, who I happily forked over dollars to. It felt good to give to those in need, to know that my graciousness would be a part of the reason they would have their stomachs filled that day. Then I arrived at McDonald's and ordered my food. However, to my surprise, when I reached into my pocket to pay for my meal, I realized I did not have a dollar left to my name. I walked back to my hotel with less than the panhandlers I had just given to.

This is a lesson that I had to be taught many times, each time becoming more and more expensive. We do it because we love to give, but without being poured back into, you will give until you find yourself completely depleted. It is especially important to note that when it is in your nature to give, it will break you even more to know that you no longer have anything to give.

The key is to stop when your tank is running low and open yourself up for the refill before you are on empty. Or to make sure that you are holding onto or existing within a structure that fills you in the ways you need. That said, stopping is the hard part. Many will consider those people and things they are pouring into before themselves. And so, to continue pouring, they find themselves distracted by someone or something that will fill or release them from the anticipated burdens of giving too much. For some, it is the external love affair that keeps them afloat, for many it is the hope of the return to a blissful past, and for many others it is a bottle of alcohol or other substances, providing a brief yet toxic vacation. Ensure that you have what you need most, or your higher self will force it. You may not like how that happens.

Know that distractions are as necessary as destroyers. As you are building or maintaining your structures, you will find yourself constantly bombarded by distractions. This is quite fine, as distractions are merely tests, unless and until you fail them. The purpose of the distraction is to let you know if you are building a structure that reflects your truest self and serving your best interests. When you are building something that you are fully vested and believe in, you will be extremely focused on ensuring its survival. The distractions will always be there and they will always be seen, but when you are invested in a healthy structure, those distractions will not usurp your attention. It is when they do that you have to give the structure immediate attention as well as examine yourself to find if you are operating in coordination with your truest self. Also, keep in mind that what a structure is to and for you today may not be the same in the future. As we change, grow, and move through our progressions, so, too, must many of our structures. Trouble arises when we try to carry something of one season into a season it does not belong. Just as the snowball will melt in the summer, so, too, will a structure that is taken into a phase of your life where it does not belong. If viewed upon as what they are, distractions can be very useful tools. When outright ignored, they can be the cause of catastrophe.

There must be feminine energy in your relationship structure. By nature, the masculine is attracted to the feminine; however, when it comes to feeling secure, he, just like the feminine, finds security in masculine endeavors. This creates a massive problem for most men, as they tend to settle, despite the fact that they have the masculine knowledge that what they truly desire is the feminine. This is a trap that you should be careful not to get caught in. Even the men who are secure enough to connect with the feminine often allow it to die in their structure as a tradeoff for gains in the area of finance. This, for the most part, began when there became a need for duel income households. There is no question that a woman should be just as free as a man to enter any part of the workforce she pleases, and to go as high in any structure as she can, but this does take a toll on the family structure. The lack of feminine energy in a household is a catastrophe waiting to happen, and that is exactly what happens when the feminine has to exist in masculine structures all day. By the time she walks through the door, she has little feminine energy left to give to her family. While she has so much to offer their structure, she is in the position of bringing into the home the same thing that he brings into the home, money. If there are children in the home, the man can almost forget about receiving much of her feminine energy, let alone real compassionate and connecting sex. For most families, it is in the best interest for the man to exist in the structure and come home to surrender to the feminine. It is also important to note that the feminine can experience a slow death by tasks that are considered menial or are undervalued by society. When she is bogged down by laundry, dishes, cleaning, and taking care of the child, she may find herself just as exhausted as if she has a nine-to-five job. To many men, this doesn't seem fair, but it is more than fair, because the reward is your delight in her energy, which is not only what you truly desire, but also it is the point of it all. Everything that you do serves the purpose of connecting with the feminine. You know this because no matter how educated she is, how much she makes, or what her title is on the job, if there is no feminine energy in the home, you will find it elsewhere.

Sometimes the right thing to do is to allow your structure to fall. There are times when the worst thing that could happen is also the best thing that could happen. There are times when we find ourselves standing at a fork in the road, paralyzed by the knowledge that neither direction is favorable. Though the paths are different, both carry the same result of ultimate destruction. At best, the benefit of one over the other is that it merely stalls the inevitable. Imagine the home that you've invested so much of yourself into is on fire. You're standing outside with the reflection of raging flames flickering in your eyes. At this point, water would only delay the inevitable; it is just a matter of time before the home is little more than charred embers. You are filled with a plethora of emotions as you envision invaluable moments made in the home and consider all that you invested in it. It hurts. But then you consider the crushing mortgage payments, the fact that you've been ready to move for years, and the neighbor that you truly cannot stand, and you think, eh, maybe this isn't so bad.

In life, we face such situations with our structures, and many times we end up as a part of those charred embers attempting to save something that was going to go up in smoke at some point regardless, and needed to. People tend to have a bad habit of clinging to the very things that are crushing and killing them. They want to save the home because of the sentimental value of it, because of how comfortable they have grown with it, or some of the things left inside, even though an attempt to save those things also requires a high risk to self. These are the people who stay in toxic relationships because they've placed too much time into it to give up, those who kill their chance at wealth by expending too much of themselves to appear that they already have it, and those who will continue to hold onto a principle, even though that principle costs them their support system and social circle.

Chapter 3

The Light

*I cannot look deeply into your
eyes without seeing my reflection,
therefore I can only see as much of
you as I can stand to see of me.*

You are standing in front of several mirrors, seeing yourself in several more.

We see very little of ourselves, and there is an irony to this that has always fascinated me. Consider for a moment your own face and the significance of it. It is the first part of you that others see, and in the very moment they see your face, so many snap judgments are reached, such as, how safe you are, your health, and how attractive you are. Whether we think of this or not, we know that every day we will be judged in an instant by possibly hundreds of people simply based on the presentation of our face. This is why we go through the lengths we do to present our faces as we hope or desire to be received by others. The moment you feel good about what you see in the mirror is the moment you feel comfortable with what the world will see, and then you're done looking at yourself. For the rest of the day, it's touch-ups and then preparing to retire for the evening. Isn't it strange that the first person you have a conversation with that day will likely walk away having seen more of your own face than you will have by the end of that same day?

Most people, especially men, don't spend much time in front of the mirror. Anything more than to prepare ourselves for the day and it gets weird. And the less we like of what we see, the less time we spend looking at ourselves in bare form, and the more time we spend working to make ourselves presentable for others. This is not an act that is exclusive to our faces; we do the same emotionally and mentally. We do it with our unresolved issues and traumas, the dreams that we have deemed nearly unattainable, our shame, our insecurities, the areas in our heart where lack of forgiveness resides, and the parts of ourselves we fear the world will judge unfavorably. We look just long enough to make ourselves presentable so no one challenges us to look longer, to peer into what is beyond the protective covering that we have created for ourselves. We run from that vulnerability.

When we don that protective covering, we are practicing inauthenticity. While in some cases it is a necessary tool, for the most part we are simply hiding from others and ourselves. We are, in effect, robbing ourselves and each other of our greatest purpose, which is self-discovery. You, too, are a mirror. But you can only be as effective at reflecting and discovering as you can be at allowing yourself to be vulnerable and authentic. How much self-discovery can a person obtain if they're constantly perpetuating an inauthentic version of themselves? How much of yourself can you discover if all you see of others is their inauthentic selves, put before you because they want you to accept them or be comfortable? Inauthenticity makes for shallow interactions and relationships. There is no depth to them, therefore no growth. This is what we have become. People who hide behind formalities, niceties, and surface-level relations, or even worse, characters who give just enough to take advantage of others.

With each person you meet, you experience a part of yourself through them, and the more rich and authentic the experience is with that person, the more you see and learn about yourself. Sometimes we meet someone who, just by their very existence, opens us up to so much of ourselves.

This is one of the reasons I encourage you to give yourself wholly, especially in your intimate relationships. The more authentic you are, the deeper you can dive into yourself, and as a result, evolve into the next progression of your whole self. At times the process will prove very painful, but isn't getting to know yourself worth the trouble?

Loving the Light was an enlightening experience, in that she, as well as the relationship itself, was a mirror that allowed me to discover more of myself than I could have ever imagined.

Most of our time together was peaceful, but in hindsight, I can see that much of that peace came at a cost. This is what happens when you suppress much of what is rumbling beneath so that you can have peace on the surface. The painful moments that we did share were some of the most intense of my life. While they were very rare, they promoted an astronomical amount of growth for the both of us.

We had something special at first sight. There was a feeling of love, there was adoration, and there was also a knowledge on my part that fate would keep us together for just a while. I saw so much feeling and emotion in her eyes the first time she looked into mine. I felt an overwhelming sense of gratitude, as well as a trembling fear as I began to really accept the responsibility of loving and allowing myself to be loved by such a person. She was a unique kind of good. The kind of good that we rarely get a chance to be in the company of in a lifetime, let alone to love. That is a hell of a mirror to catch your reflection in.

When you find yourself contemplating a new relationship, you are forced to face yourself in many ways. Forced to reexamine your strengths, weaknesses, lessons learned, life experiences, and insecurities. It is impossible to circumnavigate this, for even in the most superficial and short-lived relationship, a part of you is being exposed to yourself. If you want any semblance of a meaningful and healthy relationship, you must first find love within yourself, and how can you love what you deny yourself the opportunity to see wholly?

One lesson I gained from the relationship with the Light early on, is that when you truly throw yourself into love, or a relationship, the mirror that person is to you does not come down. It does not matter if you are thousands of miles apart or curled up on a couch together watching a movie; if you are engaged in a deep conversation about sensitive issues or taking a break from talking after a heated argument; if you are connected or drifting apart, you do not get a break from seeing the reflection of yourself in that person. Who am I when I am away from my partner? Who am I in an argument? Who am I when I feel she is fading away? Who am I after my craving to merge with her has been satiated? You cannot avoid getting to know you, although you can choose to ignore all the knowledge you have gained, at your own risk.

In my reflection I quickly found that I was not yet as ready to love as I felt she deserved to be loved, but in my selfishness, I convinced myself that I was close enough to give it a real try. In looking back, I realize that as much as the beginning felt like love, it was not. There was a lot of infatuation and more selfishness than I would like to admit. I knew that she would be a good woman who would be good for my insecurities, and that there were many ways that I could be good for her. That was enough for me to shy away from examining the gaping voids and the matter of how much the weak spots of the relationship could harm both of us at the exposure point where truth meets reality. Because the truth always meets reality. And it is worth noting that point is often where the Destroyer crashes into the structure. I was warned about this just a week before I stood before the Light at the altar, during a conversation with some friends and an acquaintance while riding through the streets of downtown Atlanta. The acquaintance, who I will call Chris, bragged about women that he was sleeping with, and on a few occasions mentioned new women he was working to conquer. Our mutual friend mentioned that Chris was getting married in just a few weeks, so I found myself confused as to how preoccupied he was with other women. I asked, "You're about to get married; are you ready to stop all of this and focus on one woman?" He replied, "Nope." I paused. *This is a huge commitment*, I thought, *how in the hell could he possibly think his marriage would survive if he keeps this up?* And so I asked another question, "Why don't you just get married when you're ready?" To which he answered, "If I were to wait until I am ready to get married, I would never get married." My mind was blown by the statement, as he was effectively saying that despite the fact that he was not ready or even remotely qualified, he was going to begin to create a structure that could crash and harm many, including the woman he said he loved. But what I could not see was that I was not qualified for marriage either, for my own reasons, and I was headed to a similar fate as him.

When I looked into the mirror, I saw the potential to be a great partner, but what I refused to see was that I could not sustain that in the structure I had built. My willed blind spot eclipsed my selfishness, insecurities, and the little boy inside of me who was always ready to cause havoc on my adulthood by fighting the ghosts of my childhood battles. The child in me needed the perceived safety of the Light, but what I needed as a man was something much different.

As most of us do, I chose to hide, which is the same as seeing with blurred vision or closing our eyes. This provides a lot more comfort than seeing things clearly, because when you see things clearly, you then have a responsibility to act in favor of yourself or from a place of love toward the person who you are in the relationship with, which is easier said than done, because in the moment, the right thing to do can be the hardest route to take.

I do not regret the decision that I made to go all in with the Light—as ill-prepared as I may have been—because the experience made me a better lover, a better man, and a better friend to myself. It made me see the significance of coming face-to-face with my insecurities rather than hiding from them, and most of all, it allowed me to realize that love and connection are all that really matters. Character is rarely, if ever, free. We have to pay several tolls to become our highest self should we choose that journey. How I learned what it means to love was a direct consequence of struggling to learn how to love someone who I felt deserved it; it was also a consequence of me deciding to love myself. There were devastating moments where hard truths were brought to light, moments that made us better as individuals while harming the structure that we were creating together.

Be the mirror. Look into the mirror.

A necessary part of evolving into your next progression as a man is to be willing to be a clear mirror, and to be willing to take a long, uncomfortable look into the mirrors in your life. To do this, you must be true and honest with yourself, and offer authenticity as much as possible, especially to the ones closest to you.

One reason men have a hard time with vulnerability is because their mind is on the next sexual conquest, rather than on evolving. They are being what they have to be in order to fuck, as opposed to being what they need to be to graduate into the next level of consciousness. If you are one of those men, I want to tell you that there is more to you than who and what you can do with your penis. Our culture has been thoroughly perverted with this toxic conception of masculinity, which ties it to sexual conquest for it to be of value. We begin to feel this as mere boys, when our budding manhood is questioned by our peers. I can easily recall being teased about still being a virgin at thirteen years old, a time where I had yet to learn much about sex. What begins as pressure becomes a need for ego nurturance and support for our own self-esteem. All of this at someone else's expense. All of which can be avoided when you realize that you are so much more. This is something that you absolutely must learn in order to contribute to yourself and others.

Your purpose here is to know yourself, and without being authentic, we deny that experience to ourselves as well as to others. While it is true that we will experience revelations about ourselves no matter how shallow the relationships or interactions may be, if we wish to have a truly meaningful experience while adding to the lives of others, then we must give, as much as we can, our purest self. This does not mean to simply not give a fuck about what others think; on the contrary, it means to give a fuck entirely. It means that with intent, you will allow growth to unfold within others and yourself simply by being authentic. This is a practice of vulnerability, which you may find terribly difficult, but know that on the other side of what you fear about vulnerability, there is rest, growth, and liberation.

Another benefit of projecting authenticity is that you attract the relationships that are truly for you. This does not mean that sustaining them won't require effort, or that they will all stand the test of time. Hardships and endings are sure and necessary. Men, just like most others, are searching for security. But most times what appears to be security only ensures your stunted growth. The type of relationships that I am challenging you to try will not always be the safe relationships you hope for. However, they will add richness to your experience of you.

Most relationships fail because people are in them with the shell of the other while they offer only a shell of themselves. And by failure, I do not mean an ending to the relationship. I am referring to the relationship exposing you to more of yourself and promoting your growth. You cannot be afraid of vulnerability if you wish to give yourself a chance to evolve and progress to new heights in life.

The type of structure the Light and I built began to fade when we were honest enough to admit that we could not offer each other what we needed, but the whole thing fell apart when we broke each other's hearts. There are few cuts deeper than the one made by the first heartbreak, and this is what terrified me about being with the Light. I always knew delivering that blow would be a part of my role in her story. From my vantage point, it was not going to be a big blow, but for one who never had to absorb one, it did not have to be big to feel titanic. I knew that it would be the nearly unbearable gift that she would need to reach her destiny. I did not come to this as a way to feel better about the hurt I caused. It was simply a knowledge from the very beginning that I accepted, just as I accepted all of the feel-good moments that I foresaw. We had all of those feel-good moments, which included growing and learning together, traveling to different countries, moving into new homes, holiday celebrations, quality time with family and friends. And then there was the moment I watched her sitting curled over in a chair, belching out tears from the depths of her soul. I had never heard her cry like that, gasping for the breaths she needed to weep while grasping at her shredding heart. The sight was horrifying and heartbreaking for me, and as much as I wanted to look away, I forced myself to see it. All of it. I needed to feel all of the pain. Her breaking heart was not the result of just that moment; it was the result of every selfish decision I had made, including agreeing to enter a marriage that I knew should not have happened just to spare her the pain and embarrassment of a cancelled wedding. I needed to feel all of it to serve as a reminder, for the next time I find myself rationalizing an act that would inevitably lead to a similar outcome.

Not too long after, it was her time to push a dagger into my heart. I did not see it coming, nor did I believe she had it in her to do, but with her own heart heavy with sadness and tears in her eyes, she caused mine to bleed as it never had. Nothing more than attraction occurred between myself and the Destroyer, but that was enough for the Light to slowly fade away as it related to the connection between her and me. She informed me that she needed a real break, and very shortly after that, she let me know there was another man. I saw it coming because I created the space for this destruction to occur, but this was still hurt on top of hurt. The final blow to a structure that was well on the way to becoming a skyscraper. After she delivered the news, I calmly wished her away, and she obliged. The moment she left, I buried my head into the palms of my hands and began to weep. Shedding tears was so rare for me that doing so felt uncomfortable. Yet as much as I tried, I could not stop them. After an hour or so of allowing myself to feel the excruciating pain flowing through me, I lay on my back, still covering my eyes. I thought: *What the fuck have I done?* I did not want her to see this, how devastated I was. I did not want her to know that I was devastated at all. But I was. It was my greatest moment of agony, and my first thought was to protect her from it. Once more, I was wrong.

    I forced myself to witness her agony, to see my reflection in her because I understood that the pain was necessary for me to reach and to be successful at my next progression. However, by robbing her of experiencing my pain, I denied her the same. I convinced myself that I was hiding my pain for her, but at least in part, I was doing it for me. I couldn't stomach the pain of seeing her in pain again, no matter what the cause of that pain was. And, I was afraid of revealing myself at that level of vulnerability. And so, in denying her the ability to see how much her actions pained me, I also denied her the chance to see how much it all mattered, and how much I cared.

For you to be the clear mirrors necessary for yourself and others to progress to the next level, you must allow yourself the gift of vulnerability. It is a masculine trait to display strength through uncompromised rigidity, especially when what is actually needed is submission to your emotional self, and this is true whether you are standing in front of the one who loves you or sitting alone in your room. The suppression of the feminine side, your emotional self is, at best, counterproductive and self-destructive. Our bodies allow us ways to release our emotional and energetic ailments, and when we deny ourselves that gift, the ailments manifest in the physical body. Holding in pain and depression, and refusing to deal with traumas both past and current, plays a significant role in men being sick, resorting to toxic substances, becoming angry or violent, and dying early. And the relationships themselves die before they get a chance to be as transformative as they had the potential to be.

Although rigidity is a trait of the masculine, the energy is not the reason men stay rigid when what they need is to surrender. In western culture, a toxic level of masculinity is often taught and celebrated. The shaming of men who allow themselves to submit and surrender to the feminine within causes other men to reject it, and leaves them with a huge void, because without that inward connection, they cannot truly embrace the feminine in another. This is what causes toxicity, misunderstanding, control, disregard, and disrespect. This, too, is the catalyst for love with a lack of connection.

She needs to see your emotional self.

She needs to experience the outpouring of your happiness, your sadness, your joy, your pain, your enthusiasm, and your emptiness. She needs to see your tears, your tenderness, your deepest fears, and your struggles, where you are weak just as well as where you are strong. What she does not need is for you to ignore or hide this part of yourself. Ignoring it will keep you from connecting with yourself and hiding it will prevent her from being able to connect with you.

Death brings new life.

At our core, what we desire is to create, which is constantly happening in countless ways on countless levels. Creation requires connection; therefore, any hindrance of the creation process will eventually cause a death. This happens in all cases because death allows for something new to arise, effectively clearing space for creation to begin anew.

I decided to enter a marriage with serious weaknesses that I chose to ignore. The weaknesses were caused by the open wounds left on the emotional and mental body of the Light by her abusive father. Voids swelled as time moved on, and the strain of it all attracted the wrecking ball that was the Destroyer. Myself, the Light, and the Destroyer will always be connected by the single point when death occurred. Death to the structure the Light cared so dearly for, death to my straining to hold it all together, and a death to the Destroyer being able to leave a demolished site unfazed. For the first time, the Destroyer had to come face-to-face with who she is and the real consequences of her actions.

We like to think about perfect moments as a point in time when everything works together in our favor and feels amazing, but sometimes the only amazing thing about a perfect moment is how painful it is. This death was a painful moment for the three of us, but the beautiful thing about death is that from it springs new life. We were all forced to see our reflection, and we were all afforded the opportunity to build a new version of ourselves and a new reality from truths left unscathed in the rubble. We were also left with the opportunity to make the same mistake again and experience an even greater collision with disaster in the near future. That is the way the cycle goes; you will have moments when you experience destructions large and small, you will either embrace the lesson, learn, and progress, or you will experience that needless and ever-growing destruction time and time again. Most of what people suffer is a product of their own creation, and even worse, it is a cycle they will repeat throughout their lives. Some go to the grave never reaching their full potential because they spent their lives stuck in the same toxic cycle that they refused to break.

If you have not already, it is time that you free yourself and move on. To do that, you must be vulnerable to be the mirror, you must be a clear mirror to reflect, you must surrender to connect, and you must connect to create. Or, you must continue to experience the death of your structures until you evolve.

Chapter 4

What Love Is

"Young man, why are you eating that fish?"

"Because I love fish," the young man answered.

"Oh, you love the fish. That's why you took it out of the water and killed it and boiled it. Don't tell me you love the fish. You love yourself, and because the fish tastes good to you, therefore you took it out of the water and killed it and boiled it." – An old Rabbi

I saw a small puppy playfully running through the bright green blades of fresh cut grass. Her hair danced in the wind and her ears flailed freely while she galloped and dashed about. She looked so happy with her tongue dangling through the biggest smile. I could feel her happiness, and it made me happy to witness it. Just behind her was a woman who appeared frantic. Apparently, the puppy had broken from the leash and she was desperately trying to hook her collar back to it. There was another puppy who was still attached to her leash, and calm. I looked to the woman and said, "She's just happy." She paid me no attention and went about the business of catching the pup. As I watched, I thought, this woman loves that puppy but what she is showing is her attachment to it. In fact, it was the attachment that made the difference in terms of what we saw and felt as we watched the puppy play. While I delighted in the puppy's play, the woman was feeling a massive amount of fear and anxiety. Because there was no present danger around, I assume that this fear and anxiety were of the puppy running off and the woman never seeing her again. The revelation I experienced in this moment is that we place a leash on who we love because we love even more what they do for us and who they are to us, and that is something we grow to become afraid of losing. What we recognize as a small threat can balloon into full insecurity, which is just enough cause for creating rules, restrictions, and structures to keep them there. Our need to control those who we love comes from a fear of losing them, when the greatest security we can ever have to keep them is simply to love them, and allow them to love themselves.

Which would you rather be, the free puppy or the one attached to the collar? Which would you prefer for the one you profess to love?

The woman felt no fear for the puppy who was on the leash, because to her, the leash provided security. But I would argue it was not necessary. Both animals are perfectly aware of who nurtures and feeds them, and play as they may without a leash, they know where to return. Ask yourself another question: Would you be more likely to leave one who delights in your liberation, or one who is only comfortable when you are bound to them in some way?

We all wish to love, be loved, and be ourselves. When we are in a relationship and one of those three elements are not there, everyone suffers, as does the health of the relationship.

Love is liberation, and the challenge of loving is allowing the people whom you love to be who they are, even when you feel some emotional and mental angst when they are doing so. Those feelings are natural; no one wants to lose something or someone that means so much to them. But to give anything other than love is to guarantee an untimely loss.

Even if you are successful in holding on to a person through control, you eventually lose what it is that you love about them because that person begins to change. The subdued pup in this story is no more than the happily free puppy on a leash. There is love, and there is the absence of love. Men have a tendency to adorn their attachment and control with a gown of love and care, so that they may feel secure while their partners suffer from compliance in silence. We even fool ourselves into believing that our controlling ways are done out of love, but love cannot be tricked into believing such a thing. At some point it will find a way to leave such an arrangement. It is time for us to be very honest about something—most men are especially good at excusing control as a product of love, and we often pay for it in many ways, such as a decrease of sexual intimacy, a contaminated environment for communication, and the death of the very feminine energy that attracted him to her in the first place.

In the opening of this book I wrote briefly of the wise women who inspired this book, giving a description of how they all relate to energy as well as their part in my story. The Coven is a group of women that

I met in a chance encounter on a white sandy beach in the heart of Florida, where I spent the night being taught by them, invaluable lessons of life, energy, the universe, and myself. It was the single most enriching and path-altering experience of my life. There were several moments that revealed enlightening lessons, but there was one in particular that changed my entire perception of women while revealing something intriguing about men. The Distraction (who differed from the one who evolved into the Destroyer of the past chapters) and of all the feminine members of the Coven had swam deeply into the ocean. It was the dead of the night, and so I could barely see them. I'm no swimmer and there were no lifeguards around, so the deeper they went, the more anxiety, frustration, and legitimate concern I felt. Though I hardly knew some of them, I felt very responsible. This is a strong trait for the masculine.

At one point they had gone so far out that I was compelled to do something about it. I yelled out to them, "You all are too far, come back!" In response all I heard was faint laughter. They seemed to be having the time of their lives out there, but they were much too far. I yelled out the same a few more times and louder on each go. My anxiety was rising, and my heart began to race. Still no reply. I felt so helpless, and even afraid. I thought of my youngest brother, who was a great swimmer, drowning a few years back after tiring out during a swim with friends. I thought about that one time as a kid when I went too far into the ocean, stepped into a ditch, and my dad had to rescue me. And then there were the what-ifs. What if one of them drowns? What if I have to watch it happen because I cannot do anything? What if the family blames me? What if I spend the rest of my life blaming myself?

After witnessing me go into a bit of a panic the Logician stood next to me. She looked out to the rest of the Coven, then back to me and said, "You're worried as fuck, aren't you?" I replied, "Yes" while still watching them as best I could. She continued, "You feel that they are in danger and you want them to come back, right?" "Of course," I replied. "They are way too far." She paused, then asked, "Do you think that they would know if they were in danger?"

I love this moment. It is forever locked into my fondest memories because it was in this moment that I realized just how irrational yet natural I was acting. I could sense the Logician looking at me, waiting for me to get it, that aha moment that most men never reach, and I did. After a long pause, I replied, "Yes…yes, they would know." I felt foolish for not understanding that the entire time. These were human beings just like me, who understood the dangers of deep waters, and even more, who could actually swim. How ridiculous of me to call them to come closer to shore where they would be safer? At the same time, I realized that my actions, though irrational, were simply a manifestation of what was occurring energetically. In my mind there was, at least, a perceived danger to the feminine, which triggered a response in the masculine to protect. Because the masculine saw itself as safe it called the feminine close to it and willed the feminine to be like it in order for the feminine to be safe as well. For the masculine, this was a win for both energies. The feminine was safe, and he no longer had to worry.

What the feminine should understand about the masculine is some of the actions they find detestable are not done with ill will or even from a place of power and control. Their actions are simply a physical manifestation of what is happening energetically. Just as the masculine should understand that what he sees as chaotic and reckless is simply the feminine living freely.

The feminine can see this in the fact that the many of the luring acts that she detests in the masculine, she is also attracted to in the masculine who has her affection. "Please come closer; the water is much too deep" sounds a lot better to a woman coming from a man who she is attached to by love.

After considering the words of the Logician I sat down onto the moist sands, crossed my legs, and continued to peer out into the ocean. As the Coven continue to talk, laugh, and play the Logician said to me, "They know where you are when they need you."

I needed to hear that, because with these realizations, I suddenly felt at a loss as to what my significance was. I needed to know, not just as a bystander on the beach, but as a man. Our culture has changed quite a bit over the last fifty to sixty years. No more are the days when having a male counterpart is a near necessity for survival. Women are free thinking, educated, thriving in the economy, and men are left asking, "What do you need me for? How am I necessary?"

The answer is: She needs you to be still and allow.

I received this answer in another moment at the beach during a dance between myself and the Feminine. With her legs crossed, she sat where the water meets the sand. As the winds pushed the waters into a rushing fit, she sang songs in the sweetest notes while she played with the water. The way she moved her body with the ocean was like a song in itself. Imagine a master of Qigong lost in the majesty of a moment, with every movement exciting the already rushing water. I simply stood directly behind her and watched with gratitude in my heart. When the crashing waves hit, they only knocked her onto me. Wave after wave came and that is the most they ever did. At one point she stopped bothering to even brace herself. She knew I was there, and as long as I stood right there, she could dance, and I could be in awe of her. It felt as though she were creating with the water, and what I gained from it, in addition to being able to bear witness, was knowing that I served a role in this beautiful process.

As discussed earlier, the masculine is stability, structure, stillness. The feminine sees this as safe, just as does the masculine; as long as this stillness is associated with love as opposed to control. Stillness with control is toxic, as stillness with love is alluring; it allows the feminine to act within its nature. When the masculine is operating in its purpose, the feminine can freely act within its own, knowing that it has a grounded point of return.

A man should think of himself as a tree, there to provide the feminine with a place of relief from the sun, and to offer fresh air and rest. The feminine will walk away and practice its liberation in the fields that surround. The masculine is terrified of her not returning (or finding another tree) so it builds fences to keep her close enough for it to feel safe. But the fence is not necessary. When she knows she has a loving and sturdy tree waiting for her, she will always find her way back home.

She needs you to be still, emotionally, mentally, physically, and yes, financially. Being still in all of these areas display an ability to provide security. Stillness does not mean that you do not have the room to change; it simply means that you are planted in areas that matter and you are standing strong.

She needs you to allow her to flourish in her femininity. As we will discuss later in this book, you, as the masculine, will not understand all of her ways, just as she will never understand yours, and that is okay. When our energy is focused on what we will never understand about our polar opposite, it does nothing more than drive the energies apart. We desire connection, therefore what we must do is appreciate those differences, understand how our partner's energy benefits them, and be grateful for how that in turn benefits us. I have not the faintest idea *why* my partner does many of the things she does, but they bring her happiness, which brings me happiness, and for that I am grateful.

Allow her to be emotional, colorful, loud, expressive, loving, full of motion, and what you may see as "dangerous." Many men will ask, "What is in this for me? Why must I suffer so much while she is so free?" You must know that we all suffer, in fact, to live is to suffer, the goal for everyone is to find something or someone worth suffering for. The feminine has her own way of suffering, whether you see it or not. Her ability to feel the energy of the earth alone is as much of a curse as it is a blessing. Do not wonder about how she suffers, instead take delight in the moments that she does not suffer, also take delight in the fact that you were the cause for some of her relief. Know that when it comes to the feminine, you will be rewarded with unquestioned loyalty and an endless depth of love, if only you give love and allow her to be.

Chapter 5

The Muse

The Muse has been perhaps my favorite teacher, because no one else dares to challenge me as she does. With flawless precision, she ruthlessly digs into the most guarded parts of me, tears so much down, and then delicately builds me up. It is always quite the surprise. But when she elects to use that skill and pour her energy into me, it is comparable to an orchestra performing an energy-shifting and mind-altering symphony. The opening is slow and methodical; we are having a friendly conversation about whatever surface issue ails me. Then the rollicking begins, an invasive round of questioning that catches me completely off guard. As the symphony moves through its crescendo, I often find myself toiling in a fit of anger and curiosity of self.

She knows exactly when to pull back, when one more step will ignite me in a way that causes our relationship to suffer. She is not afraid of that line, though. I don't even think she is afraid of unintentionally crossing it, because above all, her purpose in the moment is to be the mirror that I have a difficult time standing in front of, and this is what I appreciate about her. As the crescendo fades and the storm of emotions calms, she nurtures my fragile ego. She does with her words what a mother does with her hands after she has disciplined her child. She loves me in a way that feels good, and it reminds me that she was also loving me when it felt awful. For who she is, and the four life-altering lessons that she taught me, I will forever be grateful.

1. You are simply playing your position.

These lessons came from one discussion that lasted well throughout the night. It began with me answering a question she posed:

"Who hurt you?"

If we live long enough, we all have at least one actor in our life who fills that role; one who leaves a scar so deep that it impacts most of the major decisions we will go on to make for ourselves and many times for others.

The actor who filled that role in my story was my

mother, and I first felt the devastating blow of the pain when I was told that before I had fully formed in her, she had decided to give me away. We talked about how that pain bled over into my relationships, leading me to squander amazing opportunities with good women and hurt many others along the way. I do not wish to be the source of pain for anyone, let alone the people who choose to love me, but for the longest time, I had been breaking the hearts of others. That was never my intent, but it was almost always the byproduct of my self-sabotaging ways.

After talking through my sob story and sulking in a self-made pool of guilt, the Muse calmly responded, "You're just playing your part; we all are."

She did not tell me that I was not at fault; she did not advise me to simply move on without looking back; and she did not tell me not to care. She simply let me know that I was playing my part, just as my mother was, just as we all are. It was then that I learned that it was not my mistakes that were costing so much of my present and future, but rather the negative feelings associated with them that I had become wedded to. I did little to consider the good that came of my adoption, such as being placed into the care of the most loving parents I could ask for. Instead, I was consumed with the thought of being unwanted, which turned into constant attempts at proving myself to the mother I had never known. I had been drowning in insecurity since the moment I learned of my adoption, when I could have been full of gratitude.

For better or worse, we are always playing a part in another's story. When it's good, we feel great about it, and when it's not good, we take on the negative feelings of guilt and shame. There is a delicacy to balancing this thought so as not to end with a mindset that suggests moving through life with disregard for others is the best way to live; it is not. But what you should know is that we all will be a painful part of someone's story at some point, just as we all will experience pain at the hands of many who walk in and out of our own lives. The same goes for the good we give and receive. Life is a meaningless and beautiful song, you and all that you give are the notes that make it what it is. There is no absolute when it comes to good or bad; there is just the complexity of the song, which must be experienced in its entirety for each person to become their truest self. For each person to answer the question: "Who am I?"

Consider the pivotal moments in your own life. How has the bad shaped you? The way you answer this question depends entirely on how you choose to define "bad" and how you choose to act in the face of it. When I look back on the moments in my life when people have disappointed or hurt me, I can always find something good that came of it. Conversely, when I think of the good that people have left in my life, I can find some bad that eventually came of it.

There is a beautiful Taoist story that I want to share with you, it is of an old farmer who had worked his crops for many years. One day his horse ran away. Upon hearing the news, his neighbors came to visit. "Such bad luck," they said sympathetically. "Maybe," the farmer replied.

The next morning the horse returned, bringing with it three other wild horses. "How wonderful," the neighbors exclaimed. "Maybe," replied the old man.

The following day, his son tried to ride one of the untamed horses, was thrown, and broke his leg. The neighbors again came to offer their sympathy on his misfortune. "Maybe," answered the farmer.

The day after, military officials came to the village to draft young men into the army. Seeing that the son's leg was broken, they passed him by. The neighbors congratulated the farmer on how well things had turned out. "Maybe," said the farmer.

If you wait long enough, you can find the good in the bad and the bad in the good, or you may find that the good is the bad, and the bad is actually the good. It is all a matter of your perspective. There is even better news, you can place the titles of "good" and "bad" to the side and move about your life with intent. Plainly put, you can bend your reality to your will by making what you wish of what you are going through. Everything can be good, everything can be bad, everything can be maybe. It is entirely up to you.

As it relates to how you affect others, know that what you leave in another's life is a part of their story, and how they react to what you left in their life is their responsibility. If you leave something that you feel guilty about and you allow that to toxify other areas of your life, that is your responsibility. If something is left in your life and you choose to allow it to toxify yourself and your life, that is also your responsibility. No one person has their own story, all stories, as colorful as they can be, are caused by, affected, and intertwined with the stories of others, and when you step far enough away from it all, you can see that is so because all is one song.

2. The "need" to be worshipped by your partner is one of the greatest threats to you ever truly experiencing love.

For years, I asked myself if I made a mistake by letting a past love go. With the help of the Muse, I had come to realize the answer was no. Not because she would not have made an amazing partner, she would have, but because her part in my life was to show me what I needed in a woman, and if I should ever be loved by such a woman again, what it would be like to lose her.

The Muse asked, "This woman takes up so much space in your mind, why did you let her go?" To which I answered, "Because I was not sure if she loved me." When the Muse asked me to elaborate, I began with what I loved about the woman. I loved how she cared for me. One of the first memories I have of her is when she remarked about the paleness of my skin and made it a point to encourage me to drink more water. When she noticed that I was working too hard, she would take me to the beach, the favorite of my resting places. Sometimes she would have to fight to get me there, but she did it because she could see the stress fall from my shoulders as I gazed out into the sea's horizon. I loved how she would cook healthy meals for me, the way she looked at me, and that she would listen to me. I enjoyed it all, but there was something missing that I just could not point out, something that I just could not trust about her. *Why is she treating me so well?* I thought, *There must be some ulterior motive to this.* And so I self-sabotaged the whole thing. I let go. I did so because I was holding on to a structure that I had not evolved enough to the point of maturity to see that the structure was well worth the weight of it.

Throughout the conversation with the Muse, we initiated a search for the *why* in all of this, and within that search, I talked about how my past love was okay with letting me go if she did not feel she was getting what she needed out of the relationship, how she did not spring into action every time I wanted something, and how she didn't drop what she was doing in her own life to place me first. This is what all of my complaints amounted to. The Muse looked to the floor in thought, then to me, and said, "She loved you. Over and over again she demonstrated that to you. The problem is that you don't know love as love, you know love as worship. You're not together now because she lacked love for you; you're not together because she did not *worship* you."

I centered all of my thoughts on her words, considered everything she said, and accepted the fact that it was all true. She proceeded to teach me that this was not a me thing, but a common masculine thing. That because of our selfishness, we fail to see actual love, and instead, make the mistake of interpreting worship as love.

According to the Muse, when the masculine mistakes worship for love: *She must place him first, she must be entranced by him, he must be all that is in her heart, he must be all that she desires, she must put aside her dreams to aid in fulfilling his, she must submit to him, he must have the final say, he must be in control, and her heart must be helpless when it comes to him. He enjoys all of the languages of love: gifts, acts of service, touch, words of affirmation, and quality time. However, they alone are not enough. He wants to know that he has all of her, even when he is only giving a portion of himself.*

And then, my thoughts expanded from that relationship to all of the relationships that I had taken for granted. I had been loved by so many in so many ways, but I could never fully appreciate it. As glaringly obvious as it all was, I could not see it, and just the same as many men, I suffered the untimely demise of love time and time again.

So many have a misguided view of what love is, and because of that, it is often discounted, underappreciated, and thoughtlessly discarded. It's ironic how something so sought after can be so overlooked. In order for it to be seen and truly appreciated, a man must place his ego aside so that he may enjoy her with his authentic heart. His ego is sidelined to make sure he is filling her heart just the same. Accept this lesson and you will no longer have to spend your days searching for something that you already have.

By the time most men learn this lesson, they find themselves chasing the past, only to find that what once was is no more. She is no longer the woman who loved you, you are no longer the man she loved. You both are at different points of your progressions of life. Your past is nothing more than lessons carried into your present. Accept this and move on.

3. The need to be needed will crush you.

The need for someone to need another is either a symptom of an inflamed ego or a psychological mechanism employed for the sole purpose of pacifying one's own insecurities. In either case, it is selfish and self-destructive. For most of human history, men have been needed by women as they were most often dependent on them in many crucial ways. When a person is dependent on another for their basic needs, this places the provider in a very powerful position in that person's life. The provider may feel a comfortable sense of security, and for many, the depths of insecurity that they have within are so deep that the pressure of such a position is worth it, even when that pressure is the cause of his own slow death in the relationship.

For a long time, men did not have to consider their insecurities, nor did they have to admit to having any. Over the past five decades, there has been a major shift that has exposed this insecurity; that is women entering the workforce, demanding equal rights, and realizing their strength, therefore becoming independent of men. This is a change that caught men completely off guard and has left them wondering where their place is in an independent woman's life. As a result, many men look for a partner who needs him rather than someone who simply wants him, and who desires to love him. Some of these men even go through the process of finding someone perfectly whole, just to fuck up a part of her life so he can be what he perceived as valuable in her life by filling the hole he created.

It is very difficult to be with a whole person when you are not whole. The union itself will reveal so many insecurities. In the face of those insecurities, we have the option of either working toward a better self or begin the process of sabotaging the relationship.

The deeper the insecurity, the more inflamed the ego, and therefore the more the individual feels the need to be needed. How can a man feel and know that he is being loved when he created a reality to cater to his selfishness rather than to his heart? The Muse listened to my sorrows of never feeling loved by a woman, and gently shared that I, like most men, had not felt loved because we had not placed ourselves in the positions to actually *feel* loved, even if that was exactly what we were receiving. Men prioritize being needed because being loved with no strings attached is terrifying. The question that plagues many men: If you love me so well but you do not need me, what is stopping you from leaving?

The answer is simple: Nothing will stop her from leaving if she desires to leave, but more often than not, it will be love that keeps her there, should you dare to give it. Love is wanting your partner to be whole, and desiring that your partner can live independent of you in every way. When you are with someone who *wants* to be with you as opposed to needing to be with you, you can feel confident that it is real, and you can feel confident that you are giving your partner what she needs so she may be filled with love.

If that isn't enough reason for one to consider releasing the need to be needed, I will implore you to consider the cost of being needed. Any area of your life can be drained by another clinging to it. That newfound emptiness and pressure is often the cause of deterioration for relationships as well as one's self. Many seek relief in affairs, drugs and alcohol, longer hours at work, etcetera. All self-defeating behaviors only existing because they must be needed by another.

The security of being needed will never be worth its weight. At some point, it will fall apart in a way that it did not have to. In the face of fear and uncertainty, try love. It is the closest thing to security that you will ever find.

4. You can ask the universe for what you want, but you do not get to choose how it happens. (Include making space for the universe to give you what you want.)

I have been loved by many women, and I have judged so many of them rather than loving in return. This is the same for so many men. One of the most impactful lessons I gained from the Muse is how so many men will never experience love because they are filled with judgment toward women, especially when it comes to their past. For instance, sexuality. There are not too many women who have not been asked how many sexual partners they have had, only to be penalized for answering honestly. Still sexuality is just one of many ways. Women are judged for being "like men," just as they are judged for being "like women" and anything in between. We men love to judge, especially when we are in no real position to do so. The result of this is that women are kept locked into expectations. Men may feel that they benefit from the security of holding power over women, but where they lose, and greatly, is in the area of love. Over and over a man will find all that he ever wanted in a woman, but leave her because he does not respect the path she took to becoming who and what she is.

You can only truly appreciate who a person is when you can appreciate the journey they took to become their authentic self. This is something that men have struggled with historically when it comes to women, and their solution to that struggle has been to control the journey of women rather than deal with the real problem: their own insecurities, jealousy, and judgment. We have done our best to box the feminine into something that we deem safe for us, which comes at a sharp price for both the masculine and the feminine.

Men are the ultimate hypocrites. We live our lives and travel our journeys without any regard as to how we will be judged once we find someone along the way, but when we find that person, that is almost certainly the first thing we do.

One reason we do this is because of how society has taught us to view women, especially as it relates to their sexuality and interactions with men. This culture has two boxes for women, she's either respectable or a whore. And so, when a man meets a potential mate, he looks past what he likes in the moment to judge her through the lenses that society placed on his eyes. He may really enjoy so much of what stands in front of him, but as he learns more about how she became who she is, his perspective of what is front of him may change. Unfortunately, how he treats her usually changes with that. If he finds her respectable, he respects her. If he deems her the whore, he dismisses her or uses her for sex before walking away. Yes, it is unfair; the one who has no business judging does so, and does so harshly.

Men are not completely to blame as women often too judge other women for how they conduct themselves with men, and they too push toxic patriarchal ideals that shame women. From politics to the pulpit, women can be found shaming other women for how they choose to walk their path, and blaming them for not being able to find a male counterpart because of their ways.

There is very human element to this: the desire for security. We are all looking for it, and we have developed our own self-defeating ways to find it. The lure of chivalry is just as good at calculating how much security a person can provide as the number of sexual partners they've had in the past. Still, we cling to these things because that's what we are taught, and we can find truth in anything that we wish to believe. Before a man places his future and heart into the hands of a woman, he is going to make a calculation based on her journey, as to whether or not she can be trusted with it. He trusts the virgin, while ignoring the fact that her curiosity may be what leads her astray, while he walks away from or uses and discards the woman he categorized as promiscuous, when it was her experiences that would have been the fuel for her loyalty to him and their relationship.

Then there is a type of jealousy that is retroactive. An obsession over a person's past relationships as well as their sexual history. There are people of all kind who are guilty of this, but because of what society has engrained into men, they are especially susceptible to it. Those who experience this type of jealousy often find themselves in a loop of near-obsessive thoughts. This toxic loop creates painful emotions that lead to irrational thinking and actions, such as making their partner feel guilty about their past through constant questioning and judgments. This is a problem manufactured out of nothing; however, it can quickly turn into every reason why a relationship falls apart.

The Muse said to me, "You get to ask the universe what you want, but you do not get to choose how it will happen."

The universe will continue to bring you what you want, with a reason for you to judge your way right out of the gift that it is offering you, just to test you, to see if you have evolved out of this way of thinking and being. It will continue to gift it to you until you either turn it down to settle for what you can handle at that lower level (which will never satisfy you) or until you are able to accept its gift with love and gratitude.

These are lessons that I had to learn myself. While learning them, I realized just how judgmental I had been toward so many who I have met along my path, and how much I may have lost as a result. Not only in regard to intimate relationships, but friendships and acquaintances as well. Everyone who walks into your life comes bearing a gift whether they know it or not, and whether you are aware of it at that time or not. That gift, be it given in a moment or over a long span of time, is always invaluable. We do ourselves a great disservice when we interact with judgment rather than curiosity, gratitude, and appreciation.

What you must know how to do in order to open yourself up to fantastic possibilities in love, intimacy, and friendship, is to discard the faulty shades our culture has placed over our eyes, see everyone as being entitled to their own journey, and if you truly appreciate the one standing before you, appreciate as well the journey she walked to arrive there. Many men end up locking themselves into a relationship with women they cannot enjoy sexually, simply because he cannot cross certain boundaries without categorizing her as the whore. It's a shame, because it only leads to repressed sexual desires, a lack of connection, and many times, wandering outside of the relationship to indulge in the same sexual acts that his significant other would happily offer, and may even be starving to do so.

To recap, what I learned from the Muse that I feel will aid men tremendously in establishing and maintaining healthy and loving relationships is to:

1. Understand that you have played and continue to play your role in the lives of others. Forgive yourself for past wrongs, allow what their role in your life was to teach you, embrace the lessons learned, and move forward.
2. Release the need to be worshiped and instead see love for what it truly is.
3. Release the need to be needed. Focus on being whole so that you may share yourself with a whole person who is also willing to share their self.
4. Be grateful for the past, as it was all necessary for the universe to gift you what you asked for.

All of this requires a placing to the side of the ego and creating a comfortable space for love. It is easier in theory than in practice because to open oneself to love is to open oneself to suffering, but love is always more than worth the price it demands.

Chapter 6

Connection, Commitment, and Marriage

A man can give a woman the entire world while failing to offer the one thing she deeply desires, his unshakeable commitment to her and their structure.

In the beginning there was One.

One begged the question, "Who am I?" And so, to find out, One divided itself into two. The opposites attracted and the two reflected each other *for* each other. Because the division caused them to forget the other half, they began to remember through discovery. The two came as close to One as they possibly could, but because of the original division, they could never be One again. However, when the attraction pulled them close enough, they created another One, who went on to continue the same process when it divided itself into two. This is how it all began, the true Genesis, and this is how creation continues to unfold within, around, and to us in every way.

What attraction really is, is a desire to reconnect and be One again. You feel this when you are deeply in love with the feminine, you feel that you just cannot be close enough to her, and you find yourself remarkably curious about her story, how she thinks, how she loves, and how she views the world. This is true of the feminine as well. Men all too often miss this. We allow our egos to be fed by her curiosity and adoration, when in reality her desire to know and connect should be a humbling experience.

What we call dating and committing is just a part of the dance between the masculine and the feminine, and the point at which they connect is the point where creation occurs. Think of the point as the orgasm, and everything that built up to it as the dance. The more drawn-out, suspenseful, turbulent, or exciting the dance is, the greater the explosion when it all comes to its point. This is why with all of the problems that we face in our intimate and interpersonal relationships, it is always necessary for us to know ourselves, and for creation of all forms to occur.

Men have an atrocious record when it comes to connecting and committing, not because we are not capable, but because historically we have taken a terrible approach to both, oftentimes with good intentions.

I am going use this chapter to show you some ways of thinking that you may need to unwind, and how you can put it all together in a way that benefits your love life. The thoughts I am sharing with you are lessons that I found in my favorite symbol, the taijitu, commonly referred to as the yin and yang.

The yin and yang is a concept of dualism in ancient Chinese philosophy, and serves as a description of how opposite forces are actually complementary, interconnected, and interdependent in the natural world, as well as how they benefit each other as they interrelate to one another. It's an amazing concept of balance that has much deeper meaning than is often given credit for. Many see the light and the dark, I see the beginning, the end, and many of the answers to the deepest questions posed by man.

We will start with identifying the five parts of the symbol.

1. The feminine—the shaded part of the symbol, as to reflect the need to be filled.
2. The masculine—the clear part of the symbol, reflecting the need to be emptied.
It is the need to be emptied and filled that draw the two to each other. The need for the masculine to be emptied works with the feminine's need to be filled, as the feminine's need to be filled works with the masculine's need to be emptied.
3. The masculine within the feminine—the small clear area within the shaded half.
4. The feminine within the masculine—the small shaded area within the clear half.

This reflects that each individual is a duel energy being. Yes, as masculine as you may be, you are also feminine energy. This is good thing, and as I will explain, it is the part of yourself that you must embrace for balance and wholeness.

5. The ring—the line that traces the outside of the masculine and the feminine, reflecting the binding agent keeping the two together.

Attraction

If you have ever heard the saying "opposites attract," I am sure the taijitu gives it an entirely new meaning for you. Nothing attracts like opposites, because it is in the connection between the two that oneness is achieved. As much as there exists the desire to divide and know oneself, there is also the desire to become one again. This is the never-ending battle of the all, which is the catalyst for ongoing creation. Attraction is the easiest part, as nothing is required of you to make this happen, it is as naturally occurring with you as it is with the ladybird beetle.

Connection

Connection is the point at which the two halves come together. Be it with a new book, acquaintance, job, or love, we are always connecting. Every connection is simply a prerequisite to the next point, and this will continue until you experience the final point of your experience as you. We call this point death. Connecting with another is more difficult. You may find yourself attracted to a person only to move close enough to find there is no connection there, or that connecting to that person would not be in your best interest.

Creation

The Coven and I converged during the dawn of a spring day on a small beach in Florida, and it is from the experiences of that night that this book was conceived, and it is now being read by someone whose very existence is the product of two people coming together as one, even if it was for just that one moment. From a fresh new book to the single blade of grass closest to you, its birth, its creation, all started from a point that was followed by unique and magical paths.

What makes us so different is that we are more conscious than any other being of what we are creating, especially in terms of our realities. The career that you choose will be a major determining factor in your quality of life, who you choose to commit to will change your entire life trajectory, and while a few moments of passionate fucking may not result in a baby, it could result in a great deal of headaches. You are a creator, constantly. With every thought, word, and action, you are creating your present, your future, and sometimes you're even recreating your past. You do not have to wait to die to experience heaven or hell; you are constantly creating them for yourself right now. I created a hell when I chose to move to the dreadful north, and I chose heaven when I relocated to the shores of Florida. I chose hell every day I stayed in that toxic relationship in college, and I created heaven the moment I walked out. Again, you are constantly creating your own reality. Put the book down for a moment and ask yourself: *In all areas of my life, what hells have I created that need to change? What am I creating right now?* We are also creating for others with what we bring into their life. One act toward someone else can be the point where a sea of pain or love begins and lasts for generations to come.

The next level of connecting, loving, and committing.

Let's tie this all together, beginning with attraction. As we have covered earlier, you will be attracted to your energetic opposite, you will not understand it, and it will scare you. Nevertheless, it is for you. This is the natural way, as only the one who desires to be filled can properly drain you. There is another kind of attraction that may be just as important, and can prove to be as disastrous: an attraction to safety. Many men who are attracted to the feminine will resort to their attraction to the traits of the masculine, not because they are attracted to the masculine, but because they are attracted to what is familiar and feels safe. This is the man who sows his wild oats, so to speak, only to settle down with the woman he has judged and found safe. He knows he will suffer from boredom, he knows that he will see the end of his days being fully drained, he knows there will not be much of a dance, but he also feels confident that she will not hurt or leave him, and when it comes to settling, security is what will matter the most. This is also why he will cheat. Not because he does not love the woman he has settled with, but because he will always desire the intoxicating energy of the feminine.

You will always find yourself attracted and attracting, you have some control over this, but what you have ultimate control over is what and who you chose to connect with. People often ask me: *What is it about me that I keep attracting people who are not good for me?* I remind them that what is more important is what you accept. It is what you choose to connect with that will tell you a great deal about yourself and where you are on your personal journey. I am going to redirect your attention back to the yin and yang symbol to show you the most important factor in determining who to connect with.

What is paramount in your own personal growth and your relationships with others is that bit of feminine energy inside of the masculine half. If you are dominate masculine, like most men, you not only must acknowledge the feminine of yourself, but you must establish a connection with it. This connection may have been severed by conditioning or perhaps even by fear or resentment, but to bring you back to balance, you must have a relationship with it. The feminine part of yourself is movement, life, color, creation, and freedom, what could you possibly be without this? Dive into it. Put aside all fears of appearing weak and allow yourself to feel what is moving inside of you. Honor all of those emotions and share them with a partner whom you feel you can trust. What is also important is the fact that the feminine part of yourself allows you to have a deep appreciation of the femininity of your partner, as well as your need for her to be whole again. Without this connection with all parts of yourself, you will risk killing the feminine energy of the person you love, the very thing that attracted you to her in the first place. It's simple math. When you are only connected with your masculinity, and you connect only with the masculine of your partner, everyone and the relationship suffers, and the only thing that is created is a space for the necessary deaths of certain structures to occur.

The ring

The ring surrounding the masculine and the feminine is what keeps them bound together. This ring can be several things; unfortunately, it is most often not what it ought to be. That ring can be fear, comfort, commitment to a partnership, or the structure of marriage. What that ring should always be, however, is love.

In the beginning of the relationship, the connection makes committing very easy. It feels good, many times even magical. But as time passes, couples become more familiar with each other, insecurities and issues from the past rear their heads, fights ensue, and monotony and boredom grows. It can become a little harder for the two to remain as connected. We know this from the onset of relationships, and it is for this reason that we create arbitrary rings to protect ourselves and the relationship. Being able to say "she is my girlfriend" sends a message to all other potential suitors that she is off the market, but do you really need that title if love is the glue of your relationship? Of course not. Nevertheless, the ring feels good, comforting. Unless you are the man who wants everything the feminine or the connection to her has to offer without the ring. The ring is still there, but in such cases its usually made solely of selfishness, which itself will be a catalyst for death of the structure at some point.

Once more, there are many things that can hold the two together for a while, but only love can keep them together in a healthy way. Love is not free, nor it is easy. Those who suggest as much have never known it. Love demands forgiveness, acceptance, giving as well as receiving, empathy, compassion, gratitude, patience, and liberation. Any ring other than love was inspired in some part by fear. When you have the ring of love encompassing your relationship, you need nothing else to keep you together, including the structure that comes with the most coveted ring of all: marriage.

You should never get legally married.

Much has been said and written of legal marriage, but there are a few truths that are all too often learned in the most unfortunate way, most times leading to catastrophic meltdowns of relationships that could have otherwise stood the test of time. A legal marriage can be beautiful, but it is mostly just disastrous. The facts do not lie on this, as not only do the great majority of them end in divorce, the burden of the institution on a relationship itself often leads to mental, physical, and emotional health problems as well as self-destructive habits that harm all involved. The irony of it all is that none of this is necessary. To marry another is to wed yourself to that person, and all that is needed for that is commitment of the highest degree between you and your partner. What we have been indoctrinated to believe is that to commit at this level, we have to wed a perfectly fine relationship to a government institution. And that is what legal marriage is, you and your partner making the government a third partner in your union. What we are saying to ourselves when we do this is that we are not capable enough to manage our own relationships, therefore we need government regulation to make it work.

What legal marriage really is.

Legal marriage is one of our most prized structures, and this structure has many layers to include the judicial system, spiritual or religious beliefs, finances, and cultural/societal norms. All of them are designed to keep in those who have walked inside and locked the doors. This is the appeal of marriage. As with most structures, the purpose of it is to provide a sense of security, that no matter what the couple goes through, one person is guaranteed by these structures that the other person will not leave because he or she "cannot" leave. Especially after all that we go through in dating, it is comforting to know that you can pour your all into something without the fear of it disappearing at a moment's notice. Of course, marriage cannot actually provide this, but that is what it is sold and bought as, and even with its abysmal failure rate, we continue to fall over ourselves to sign that supposedly lifelong contract with our significant other because few people consider the tremendous amount of pressure that the relationship immediately takes on when wedding it to this structure. Once you sign that legal document, the relationship that was perfectly fine is instantly buried under crushing religious, societal, cultural norms and expectations. The very things that are designed to keep you in the marriage become the same things that will make you want to get the hell out of it. I get it, you have a beautiful thing that you want to preserve. What I am relaying to you is that it would do your relationship better service to drown it in love rather than unnecessary stressors.

In unpacking the reason why we value marriage, we can see the reason it was created. The chaotic dance between the masculine and the feminine are constantly being manifested. Just about every relationship issue that we have can be traced back to the characteristics of each energy. Men are constantly trying to control women because this is what the masculine understands—control, all else is chaos. However, he is wildly attracted to this chaos. This is why he cheats on his loyal wife with the wildly free woman. Women desire to see their men open up, to let loose emotionally, and be free. They want him to experience the fullness of life as she does, but of course not too much, because she is also attracted to the security of him being still. If she is the wind, he is the tree that she dances through and around. In the midst of a storm, he is the calmness to where she can find refuge. Without this stillness, this masculinity, she will leave to find another who can provide it.

It is in our nature to have as much strife as we have harmony and as much conflict as we have peace, as this is the formula of creation. And so, marriage was created to place a gate around the two, to serve as a boundary, saving them the pain of separation as a result of their own nature. When the gate was not enough, marriage became a fortress, furnished with governmental incentives and locked by legal, financial, cultural, and religious penalties.

Marriage is not some evil institution, but rather a solution to a problem. The issue is that with every solution to a problem, another problem is also born, in some cases a multitude of problems are born. A man wishes to marry to solve the problem of being alone, and in doing so, he invites all of the problems that come with wedding himself to another and the institution of marriage. Over time, the man finds that marriage is just not worth the problems that it presents, so he decides to solve the problem by divorcing. In enacting that solution, he creates a multitude of new problems that include hiring a lawyer, parting ways with much of his assets, suffering the emotional toll of the break, being apart from his children, starting over and so on. The question is always: Is it worth it? Not the marriage itself, but the problems that will be gained along with those benefits we love so much.

I would also argue that many men should not marry because the masculine is so distracted by the feminine, it is not in their nature to be successful in such a rigid structure. We know this to be true because many men have fallen victim to their own masculine nature regarding the unquenchable desire to release with more women than one. However, it is an adherence to the structure that saves him from himself and the unfortunate fate. Many will argue that it is not in a woman's nature to tie her free-flowing self to such a rigid structure as well, after all, how free can she be if she does?

She, too, is then bound in so many ways, especially as it relates to expression of her feminine nature. Too much of that and she will instantly be judged against the idea of what a wife should be. Still, the structure saves her as well. It provides at least some security that she will not have to endure the extreme hardship of raising her children alone, as well as some relief (hopefully) from the trials that come with dealing with carousel of men who will, at the least, waste her time.

Divine Marriage

The definition of marriage is *to meet* or *to blend with something*. We can do this in a number of ways, but the greatest and most divine way we do this is by creating a child. A child created between two is the ultimate marriage. You can walk away from a ring, a piece of paper, or a verbal commitment, but a child is forever, and the marriage is even deeper when this creation is done so with intent. Even more, a child created between two is the closest that two people can come to one, our ultimate desire. When you merge with another and create a child, you can see the two of you in the one being in ways other than and including the physical. This is true, divine marriage. The ultimate connection.

Divorce

The real value of marriage is in how difficult it is to get out of, and that is what divorce offers. It is, in fact, the signature piece of the institution. That's right, when you marry legally, you are not committing to life with another so much as you are placing a bet with nothing to gain but a whole lot to lose. On your death bed, you get to brag that you were married for forty years, but you can do the same without the legal documents. If you ever walk away from the relationship, it is worked out between yourself and your partner; however, if you walk away from a legal marriage, the government will make you pay dearly. It's a raw deal, and I will share with you a portion of my taste of it.

    I had about three minutes to make it to courtroom 3E, thanks to congested traffic and a faulty GPS app. The Light wasn't making it much easier by franticly sending me texts asking where I was and informing me that the courtroom officer was calling my name to check in for attendance. I checked my watch. Two minutes to go and they were not allowing anyone aside from jurors to enter the elevator. Great, I thought, as if the weight of a divorce were not enough, I had another reason for my heart to pound out of my chest. I checked my watch again. One minute left before I would be too late; finally the elevator door opened to take me from floor two to three. How could there not be a staircase for that? Ridiculous. The elevator three button lit up, the doors opened, and I dashed out. The Light was standing outside of the family court room appearing to be frustrated with my just-in-time arrival. I was more than surprised when I entered the room to find the judge, an officer, and three rows full of people I had never seen before. We took our seats in the front row. The loud thuds of my heart pounding against my chest slowly calmed, giving way to the stale energy and uncomfortable quiet of the room. I looked over to the Light and noticed the tears begin to fall. I assume she felt what I was feeling: embarrassment, shame, and the pain of a death that many never saw coming. For months we lived our lives independent of one another, thinking little of the impending legal process, but on this day, there was no way to deny the pain of extreme loss as we pulled the plug and watched what little was left of that relationship take its last breaths.

The judge finished up her ruling to honor another divorcee her request to retake her last name, then she called us to come to the tables. The bailiff placed us opposite of each other, as though this was a her vs. him situation. I looked over to the Light, who was on the verge of breaking down into tears, and for a moment I thought about the life that I had shared with this person. I thought about the joyous point wherein we stood together in front of our friends and family and said "I do." And this point, sitting across from each other in front of a judge and a crowd of strangers, telling the court that there was nothing that could be done to save the marriage. Before I knew it, the judge ruled that our marriage had been dissolved. It was not until that moment that I realized in legally marrying, all we did was wed our relationship to a governmental structure for regulation. We had agreed to split several months prior, but the relationship could not be severed without this government approval. It was a relationship of three rather than two, myself, the Light, and a structure that predated us by hundreds of years. And it was that third actor in our relationship that nearly tore our friendship apart as well.

 I held myself together throughout the process, but it was the hardest six minutes and thirty-seven seconds I could remember enduring, and through every second of that time, I cried inside for it to be over. Separating was hard, but it was something that we accepted and allowed us to remain close. It was the process of going through a divorce that nearly ripped us apart. It is supposed to be this way. It is the lock that makes marriage so alluring. But it is also unnecessary in that people should be able to walk away from something that no longer works for them without the government making them go through an excruciating and invasive process. It's something you never have to deal with if you choose to stay away from the institution all together. You do not need the government to stay together, you just need love.

Whether you marry legally or not, commit.

By no means am I advising you not to commit to someone who is good for you, you absolutely should. Through the pain of loneliness, we can surmise that we are not here to be alone. Whether you choose to wed your relationship to the legal structure of marriage, or you choose instead to agree on that level of commitment between yourselves, committing yourself to a good partner and a healthy relationship can have tremendous benefits. Deeply committed relationships, specifically marriage, has been good for men as it has a history of making us cultured and civilizing us. It also gives us more to think about than ourselves. We become protectors and providers who consider more than our own desires; we become invested in our legacy. Such commitments also provide a continuity of narrative, reproductive success/child rearing as a team, achieving a deep level real intimacy, having someone to share amazing moments with, and enjoying the pleasure of wholeness. There is nothing more valuable than such a connection, and whenever there is a chance to have it, it should not be taken for granted. It is the opportunity of a lifetime to experience such a bond, and I hope that it is something you choose to relish in if you have not already.

But it must only be with one. As a dominant masculine being, you are cursed in many ways. A trait of the feminine is variety, and your unending desire to release will include an unending desire to be drained by multiple partners. The desire alone may cause your brain to reward you with a taste of euphoria, but to indulge in untamed lust, greed, and infidelity will most likely cost you a lot more than what it's worth.

A disciplined and honorable man will never cheat.

To be disciplined means to have a controlled form or way of working. It is the disciplined and honorable man whose way it is to stand the winds of all distractions to remain loyal to his partner. He can do this because he has chosen the one for himself and because he cares for how his actions affect her as well as the structures they are building and maintaining together.

There are many penalties for infidelity, and the severity of some of those penalties can be devastating. Even entertaining my attraction with the Destroyer left my structure in ruins, but what hurt much more was losing the way the Light looked at me. When you really hurt someone, you can see the pain in their eyes. A place within them that was once filled with love and adoration, can, in a moment, be emptied and replaced with repulsion, disappointment, and anger. You can find the same in the eyes of your parents, your friends, your children, but even worse, you may find it in your own eyes when you look into the mirror.

Cheating is not free. It robs. It robs your relationship of trust, respect, and a connection that was once so pure. It breaks the relationship. Even if the couple stays together and are able to build something new from it, it will never be the same.

There is no reason to cheat. There is no reason to cost yourself so much. Not when there is the truth, which is there to set you free. Cheating is only enticing when there is something missing, whether that something is in you, in the relationship, or something of importance that you are not receiving from the person you are with. Before you engage in infidelity, try using the tool of honesty. Be honest about what is missing and then give that gift to yourself as well as your partner, then make sure the actions that follow are in line with your highest self. Sometimes the truth sets us free of people and things that we do not wish to let go of, but if it was the truth that caused the separation, it was meant to be for a better you.

In Chapter 4, I shared an experience at the beach with the Feminine, wherein I learned that in order for her to create I needed to be still. There is more to that story that holds another very important lesson. Just a few feet away from me lay the Distraction. A beautiful woman who was herself distracted by her phone. As long as I stood perfectly still, the Feminine could continue creating, uninterrupted by the small waves that crashed against her. They would do little more than knock her into my legs, as from time to time I would move them into her way to stop her from toppling over. Whenever I looked to the Distraction, I would look back to find that I missed a moment that the Feminine needed me to move in a certain spot behind her to keep her from falling. Her creating was interrupted any time I paid attention to another woman. The Logician, who knew that the idea was something I was entertaining, walked up to my left shoulder and said, "You see, even if you could love two women, your relationships would suffer from you being divided. When your attention is off one, the other falls, and when you are not playing your role, the Feminine cannot create."

The reason why many women see their progress in life so interrupted is because they are sitting in front of a distracted man. When you truly care about the person you are with, as well the progress they have the potential to meet on their path, you do not wish to be a distraction from that, you want to help her make it.

We have always pondered the question, what do women want? The answer is simple: They want you to be still. You can have as many women as there are women who want you, but you can only build wholly with one woman at a time.

Chapter 7

The Healer

We are the freest that we have ever been, and yet many of us remain blindly controlled. Not by any god, nor even any man, but by the younger self, who sits on the throne of our mental and emotional bodies. We navigate throughout our paths, thoughtlessly tied to puppet arm rods, dancing to the tune of the master, a child who never quite got over traumas endured.

It was not until my thirties that I realized the major decisions I made in my twenties were a direct consequence of what happened to me in my younger life. I realized the freedom I thought I enjoyed was no freedom at all; I was being controlled the whole way. I enlisted in the military to serve as proof to the mother who gave me away that I was worth keeping. I courted women into falling in love with me, only to serve as proof to those sixth-grade girls who taunted and rejected me endlessly that I was worth a flirt back. I went to college to prove to my family, who laughed at a kid who said he could earn a degree, that I could dawn that prestigious black robe and walk across the stage. I accepted all that what was done and said to me as an indictment, and I had dedicated so much of my youth building a case against them for myself and a host of people who by then had probably forgotten my name. From large decisions to small, I could offer a buffet of those who were governed by my younger self, and if you take the time to think about it, you can too. This is not to say that it's all bad; much of who we are is shaped by what we have been through. It is simply a question of how one wishes to live their life. The forks in the road present several possibilities, the directions we choose to walk typically boil down to whether we will truly live our lives for ourselves or walk a path of endless battles with ghosts of the past.

The Healer knew exactly where my pain was. I was astonished by this, until I realized that my pain rested in the same place that it does so many other men. It is somewhere in our boyhood, at the moment when our hearts were bruised by one of our first loves and we subconsciously decided to shield ourselves from such a pain by almost any means moving forward. Initially, we feel ourselves victorious when it comes to escaping the pain that comes with the tumultuous dance between the masculine and the feminine, but it is our partner who suffers, often finding herself taken for granted and unloved. While we can dodge the pain, we, too, must pay. The bill is due when we realize how much more grand the dance could have been had we submitted ourselves to all of it.

But we often only learn after the damage is done. After we have moved through much of our best years trampling hearts earned and given, always knowing that we would only give so much in return. As a consequence, we find ourselves in opposition to our nature. After a lifetime of withholding his love and emotions, the masculine, who desires to be empty, finds himself full of that which he has suppressed. While the feminine, who has given too much, stops to find herself drained, devoid of anything to offer for herself. Neither can exist in such a way. It is at this point where the two must experience a break, if for no other reason than to know that they are operating against their higher self.

We have to take responsibility for our part in this toxic cycle. While it is true that our teacher is a society that promotes a rewarding of toxic masculinity and denies us tools to aid in being expressive and loving, once we understand this truth, it is our responsibility to do better, to connect with the feminine, the healing part of ourselves that we have so long denied.

When we learn of the personal cost of our fear of vulnerability, withholding our love and a life of suppressed emotions, we are left with a world of what-ifs rather than possibilities, and the grief of knowing that we may have played a tragic role in someone else's life, and it did not have to be that way. It truly is a vicious cycle, one that if ended earlier could mean all the difference in the world for love and relationships. What if a hurt man could identify his toxic actions and understood the endless waves that they create in the lives of others *before* he ruined the love of his life or felt the paralyzing fear of his baby girl being hurt by a man like him? It is safe to say that our culture would be a lot different; at the very least, it would be much more accommodating for healthy relationships.

However, the Healer is not as interested in saving the world as she is saving a particular soul. The Healer's eyes were as beautiful as they were piercing, but I hated how she could see right through me, how she could feel what I felt before I had the chance to lie to her. As she tore through my defenses and sought the source of my pain, a few words slipped out that I had never uttered before: "Why did she leave me?" When she saw the first tear roll down my cheek, she wrapped her arms around me in a tight embrace. Before I knew it, I was purging through a full-on cry. It was as if everything I was supposed to release since finding out that my biological mother gave me away came out in that moment. After I soaked her shirt with my tears, she took a small step back, looked up into my eyes and rested the palm of her hand gently onto my chest. In a voice as calming as the wind sprinting across an ocean shore, she said to me, "You don't have to hurt us; we are not your mother." In our relationship, she experienced the pain that I took in when I learned that my mother gave me up for adoption. It was as though she was speaking on behalf of every woman I would ever encounter, a plea to save them from that same pain transferred to them. It was as if she were speaking to every man on behalf of every woman, saying, "You do not have to give us the pain that has been given to you." It was not the first time I heard that, it just touched me differently because it was the first time it was directed toward me. For years I had been working with women who were left broken as a consequence of trying to repair broken men, or trying to be a mother to the ones who never had one. The sick will always find the Healer; unfortunately, the result of that is sometimes the Healer becomes sick too. There I stood in front of the Healer, still sick, and if I had not allowed myself to accept what she was saying to me, I would have risked making her sick too.

I thought I released all that pain years ago. I forgave my mother and had begun to see things from a different perspective. Rather than harping on the thought of her giving me away, I began to cling to much better thoughts, such as the fact that she carried me to term when she had other options, and the incredible family that I was placed with. I thought I was long past it all, but I came to realize that all I did was change the narrative, I never released the pain. The hurt was still there, and even more, there was a fear of experiencing any relatable pain again. It did not matter that I was unaware of the turbulence within; it was affecting me, my capacity to love, and the ability of others to love me without being burned in return. Being distant, sometimes cold, emotionally unavailable without the courage it takes to truly let someone in. It was all there. I may not have been aware of it, always assuring myself that I was good enough, despite not returning the favor of risking my heart, but they knew, and they suffered as so many do when either or both of the dance partners are plagued by fear.

I did not want to accept the words of the Healer. I did not want to think about the pain and the resentment I was carrying, and I surely did not want to think about how those negative feelings could be harming people I genuinely cared for. For the most part, I believe this is the conundrum that many of us find ourselves tangled in, a repetitive cycle that involves hurting ourselves by hurting others through the actions tainted by the hurt within. This is just one of the ways that we cause our own suffering and exacerbate the suffering that we cause others.

In the most privileged time to be alive, we can speak as we want, go where we please, eat whatever we crave, settle where we dream, create as we are inspired to, and live as we wish. So then, why do we still experience and cause so much pain? If you take an honest look at the issues you are facing on a daily basis, you will find it was you who created them. If you look even deeper, you will find that most of those pains are directly related to the battles that you lost as a child. Those traumas do not stay in our childhoods, and how could we expect them to, being that they are the very foundation upon what our adulthood is constructed? The traumas don't just bleed over, they pour over, playing a significant role in our thoughts, beliefs, and actions, and it is our thoughts, beliefs, and actions that create our suffering.

When I learned that my mother had given me up, I felt unwanted by the woman who should want me more than any other being on this planet. I do not know why she gave me up, but knowing that she did created a deep void within me. I grew to need that constant validation from women, and because that hole inside of me was linked to a woman who only exists in my mind, the hole itself became an unfillable vacuum of pain. While my intentions and my feelings would be in the right place, I would often find myself walking away whole from a person I had left broken. And as much as it hurt me to hurt others, I would not feel right if I did not feel her pained by my departure from her life. The way I understood it, if there was no pain in the separation, my presence was of little to no value to her. Above all things, I had to feel valuable, and I was willing to be a ball of pain for others in order to feed that to myself. During my time therapizing men who had a history of domestic violence, I learned how typical it is for men to lash out with some type of violence when they feel cornered and overwhelmed by their own pain. Insecurity, jealousy, heartache, worries, unresolved traumas, and fears are all released as violence against others, and many times in forms carefully disguised. For many men, all of that pain is manifested into control and sexual conquest, for me it was taking just enough to feel wanted. That was more than enough to harm those who only wanted to love me.

That's my story. Everyone has their own, sometimes even a whole host of them. Our pains are like seeds that have the ability to grown into trees, or they can be blunt force traumas that bear nothing more than additional misery. The pain that men have experienced becomes the pain that we give, and there is so much of it in this world. This seems to be the case for three specific reasons.

First, many tend to invest more into protecting themselves from being hurt again rather than forgiving. While protection is necessary, and a matter of survival in many ways, it becomes toxic when it turns into isolation, defensiveness, minimizing, denial, and blame. With the goal of protecting ourselves from harm, we curl our emotional bodies into a fetal position, blocking pain from outside sources while stunting our own personal growth. So much energy is being placed into protecting ourselves from others that we do not realize our methods of doing so may lead to more pain being caused to us *through* the pain we give to others. An example of this is a woman leaving because she is not receiving the intimacy she has been begging for, or a man closing off the part of himself that his woman loves in response to her locking a key piece of her heart away.

Forgiveness demands that you let things go that you may not wish to let go, especially when you know they are hurting you. The courage that you need for a healthy relationship demands that you open yourself up to the possibility of being hurt again.

Remember, you deserve to have the burdens of anger and resentment lifted from your shoulders, and there are times when that lifting will have to be done by you alone. It is a liberating experience that opens you back up to love, growth, and yes, pain. Still, I would encourage forgiving and remembering as oppose to forgetting. You are thankful for the lesson, that does not mean you want to live through it again.

Secondly, many of your pains and traumas are at best, secondhand. These are the traumas that we did not experience directly, but still harm us, and that we carry on to others. They are the traumas that happened to our parents, our friends, intimate partners, and even strangers. It is amazing to think that something that happened to someone you do not know, generations ago, can be the source of your pain today. I know that I inherited my emotional guardedness from my father, who inherited it from his father, who was emotionally injured when he was a child in an event that is mostly unknown to me. The direct trauma did not happen to me, but the Light felt the results of it through me during our entire first year wedded, and it depressed her. Not knowing my biological parents is the source of my deepest pain. There is a story as to why there was a decision to give me away that I do not know, and behind that story is likely a trauma that I will only know the damaging effects of.

Look within, examine your wounds, and find how many of them actually belong to you. I was able to move past many of these traumas not only by acknowledging their presence in my story, but also their role in the parts of me and my life that I really enjoy. I love who I am today, and my journey to this point is just as responsible for who I am as how the journey began. My deepest trauma is also the birthplace of my deepest joys. This has always been the case, but it only became my reality when I chose to see it. You have the power to do the same.

Lastly, we cling to our pain. Learning the pain I was giving was the result of my adoption was not enough for me to change right away. After all, change is rarely warranted or easy, even when it is the best thing for you. I did not change because I knew it would be hard, because I knew it would require some real inner work, and most of all because I enjoyed what I received from it even though it hurt others. Sounds terrible, but we all use what works. I needed validation from women to soothe and fill that gaping void, and I had perfected the art of gaining that. All I needed from them was to feel wanted, the moment a desire for anything more appeared, that was my cue to act ignorant of the entire matter and disappear. For a time it was subconscious, but learning the what and the why only compelled me to become more skilled at it. This is because along with it feeling good, by disappearing, I did not have to see how my actions affected others, and I did not see how they were affecting me. It was not until I started to see people's value beyond the holes they can fill that I began to stay around long enough to see the negative effects of my actions. I learned that we cannot hurt others without hurting ourselves. Not only was I harming women who developed real feelings for me, I was harming myself in that I was robbing myself of potential connections with amazing people. There are many reasons people cling to their pain. Sometimes it is the guilt of moving on, sometimes it is the anxiety attached to change, and sometimes they feel so justified for feeling pain that the pain becomes their crutch. Sometimes people just want others to feel what they are going through. The reasons are endless, but none of them save us from the self-destructive side effects of holding on to our traumas, as that alone is an illness in itself.

Though the cycle of experiencing and giving pain is ongoing and not at all desirable, there is a reality to it; it is necessary. Pain is necessary for growth, and it is a necessary tool for safety. It is also a necessity for all paths in order for the sojourner to actualize his or her full potential. Still, we have a responsibility to ourselves, not only in giving ourselves as little pain as possible, but to also extend that favor to all we encounter.

While we are all guilty of doling out pain, men's ways of addressing their pain can be problematic and even catastrophic. Men have a privilege that allows them to move through much of life completely oblivious to the harms they cause, such as the way I did to fill my need for validation. There are a few ways in which we must evolve in order for a needed shift to occur in our culture.

Carnality

You have a need to be emptied. That root force to release that you always feel is a constant call for creation. In other words, that magnetic pull to be inside of a woman is for the two of you to come as close to oneness as you possibly can so that you may create one, a child. The draw to merge with a woman is insatiable and never-ending, because creation is insatiable and never-ending. As a co-creator with the all, this is your gift and curse as the masculine, as hers is to be filled.

Unlike other animals, we think more deeply about procreation and what that means for our own experience in life. Therefore, on many occasions, sex is just a means to satiate that desire for a while, so we use whatever tools at our disposal to avoid creating a child. However, child or not, we are always creating something. Because this desire is so demanding, and because being truly united with the feminine requires a cost many men are not willing to pay, what is often resorted to are lies, manipulation, and games. To use such tactics to bring ourselves relief is to operate at the lowest levels of our being. At this level we are operating in pure selfishness. We are always in a state of creating. While we may not be creating a child, in such scenarios we are creating destruction for those we are using as well as ourselves.

Women have to be seen as more than a tool to satiate our sexual urges. Once more, you will always have the desire to merge with multiple women, but you should understand she is a human who deserves your decency, and that if she allows you in, she is allowing you access to the most sacred place on earth: the womb, where all human life begins. It is only then that we can truly appreciate the divine nature of creation and the feminine. A man must see that the fulfillment he desires is much more than physical, it is the point where the masculine meets the feminine. It is the way in which creation occurs and that desire is a call for him to fulfill his divine purpose. When he knows this and has gratitude for divinity of it all, he can place his carnality to the side and instead allow his actions and words to be governed by honesty, transparency, humility, and respect. Women are the gatekeepers to reproductive success. Without them, we would not be; without them, there would be no continuity of our genes; and without them, there would be no divinity to the masculine. The feminine deserves nothing less than the very best of the masculine.

You have more to offer than your penis.

For about three years, I facilitated group therapy sessions for men who were returning to society after being incarcerated for domestic violence. Our goal was to give these men the tools needed to thrive in a healthy relationship. As any decent therapist would, we searched for the baseline of our clients; we wanted to assess where they were in order to aid them in their journey to become who they needed to be to exist in a healthy relationship. One of the first things that I learned from these men was their commonalities regarding sexuality.

Nearly all of them saw women as little more than what my supervisor referred to at the time as "sperm depositories." Meaning, they saw little use of women outside of sex, and often treated them as such. The men bragged about their conquests, how little work they had to put in, how many children they had (whether or not they were caring for them), and how many women they were playing. I realized that a man will give a woman what he feels he has to offer, and if all a man feels like he has to offer is the ability to fuck and make children, that is all that he will give. Remember that no matter what position she has in your life, she is still a mirror. What you give her says more about you than it does about her, and if all that you have to give is sex, then you are operating at the lowest level with a lack of awareness as to how divine the act of sex and the feminine are. The knowledge of this alone will inspire you to evolve and become more, simply because at this mental place you understand that she, as well as yourself, are owed it.

Reproductive Privilege

One of the greatest privileges that men have is not having to hear the ticking of our biological clocks as loudly as women. Should we desire to someday have children, we do not have to consider finding a suitable mate as much, and needing to do so while we are still reasonably young. This is what women have to go through. While they are just as sexual as men are, they have to be a lot more responsible and they have to get to that point a lot quicker than we do. Every man should keep this in mind so that he understands just how selfish he is being when he is wasting her prime years with his games, immaturity, recklessness, and selfishness. We often talk about marriage as the ultimate goal, but marriage is just the structure created to provide what we really want. For her, it is a safe and secure environment so that she may, along with other desires, fulfill her part in the divine point of the dance between the masculine and feminine.

You must progress to the next level or move out of her way. Everything that she wants in life, including the dance, may be right after you. You may not be ready for that level of commitment, or perhaps she is not the one. In any case, it is a sign of an evolved man to step aside and allow her to be. It is also an act of love.

Power and control

Some the more notable ways that men cause trauma to women are found in methods used to establish power and control. These methods include, among many more, verbal, psychological, and financial abuses. And when those fail, there is the final safeguard of physical abuse. These tactics are what unevolved men resort to when they come face-to-face with their greatest fears: powerlessness and separation.

Men love and hate nothing more than the feeling of being powerless. They hate it because it forces them to submit to the will of another, and they love it because it is from the place of submission that they find excitement and purpose in the pursuit of power. This is why we love the chase of women, because there is no greater kryptonite to the masculine than the feminine, therefore there is no greater joy than to catch her. This is the natural way, but of course there will always be those who cheat the game because it is much easier to have your way when you are in a secure position of power over those who you know have the ability to weaken you.

In one of my previous books, *It's Okay To Let Go*, I shared an instance of religious abuse that continues to add to the oppression and forced submission of women. In the very beginning of the Christian Bible [Genesis], it establishes man's rule over woman in two ways. First, man is created before woman, and woman is created of man, therefore placing him at higher regard than her. We see this made clear in 1 Timothy 2:11: *"A woman must learn in quietness and full submissiveness. I do not permit a woman to teach or exercise authority over a* man; she is to remain quiet. For Adam was formed first, and then Eve." Never, in the history of natural birth, has a man been created in anything other than a woman's womb, and yet here we have a perversion of creation. The placement of this absurd story demonstrates just how imperative it was to establish power over women in the early church. Just to clarify, not only did woman not come from man, but the ova (the woman's egg) came before the sperm, as she was born with them while your sperm are constantly being created on a sixty-four-day cycle. That means that you are not first in anything, and when it comes to the creation process, your contribution is quite small. You are only needed for conception, while the woman carries and births the child. So, if we are picking the power order based on creation, we've got things a bit backwards.

Then there is what we are all familiar with, the original sin, when after eating the forbidden fruit, God cursed all wives to be ruled by their husbands, Genesis 3:16: *"To the woman he said, 'I will make your pains in childbearing very severe; with painful labor you will give birth to children. Your desire will be for your husband, and he will rule over you.'"* One would think that a merciful God would show a little more compassion, especially if he were to take into account that Eve was basically an infant who was tricked by the greatest deceiver of all time. But the point of these stories is not to be rational, they are to establish male power and control in a way that cannot be questioned.

Separation, to the surprise of many, is the deepest trepidation of men. What we experience on the surface is the perpetually manifesting core of the masculine, the fear of the feminine leaving. There is no greater pain for men, which is why they will go to toxic lengths to ensure it is a pain they never have to experience. The masculine is stillness, which also means that it represents an end, a period, a full stop. The dance of the one splitting itself into the masculine and feminine has been ongoing since antiquity. It is a constant process, the catalyst for all of creation. However, the masculine is exhausted by the process. At times it is so broken it no longer wishes to participate; to separate itself from its better half. It knows the pain of it all, but it just wants it to stop. But its capture of the feminine curses it, just as does peace curse humans. We enjoy it, we grab ahold of it for dear life, then we forget why and destroy it all. We destroy the connection, we destroy the peace, we destroy Eden, just to remember all over again. Thus, creation. The masculine wants to stop because separation is so painful. This is where the desire for control comes from in men, it is actually a deep desire to stay whole, so that it does not have to feel that pain again.

Being that we are a small piece of the whole, that pain is energetic and at our core. It is the first pain and the deepest. Therefore, the feeling is understandable, whereas actions involving the establishing of dominance over another are not excusable. What a man should understand is that the feminine cannot and will not be contained by force, because even if *she* is kept by force, her femininity will either die, be withheld, or given to another. He should also know the only thing he can do to keep the feminine is stare that fear in the face and risk losing her by allowing her to be free. That is love, and love is the closest thing to security that we will ever feel.

Before you do anything, stop.

When I realized that my actions were causing pain to people who only wanted to know and love me, all I knew was that I wanted it to stop. I did not know where it all came from or how to end it, but I knew that it was not who I wanted to be. While pain is necessary, it was not the gift I wanted to give if I could help it. Therefore, I took a pause. I took a pause from dating, flirting, befriending, and every action that I felt would inevitably lead to someone being harmed. I stopped so that I could observe myself. I needed to learn not only the what, by the why and the how. It was an extremely difficult stare into the mirror, but once I moved past the pain, the healing began to occur. Before you do anything, stop. Be compassionate to the child within and offer forgiveness to yourself as well as those who have harmed you. See the way your actions are hurting those you care about, including yourself, and do the work necessary to heal and evolve. It is not easy, but it is worth the trouble, and it is essential.

Chapter 8

Intimacy and Loving

In the early days of our union, right after the clouds of euphoria began to dissipate, a few threats to this seemingly perfect relationship involving myself and the Light were being revealed. The most significant of them all being the level of intimacy that she needed of me to achieve the closeness she so desired. I was oblivious of such a need even existing, and I, like most men, had little clue as to what intimacy is and its significance, especially to the feminine. During our first year bound to each other, I was by far more of a functioning program than I was a lover. This program was a product of a lifetime of lessons about who and what a man should be, specifically as a husband. Just like many, I was taught that the man should be the head of his home, his job is to be the provider, and as it relates to this subject, he should always appear stoic, even when he is crumbling inside. Much of what I learned about what a man should be came from religious ideology and what I witnessed of my father and his father, as well as what I saw of the women in their lives and their acceptance of it all. We are constantly being inundated with ideas of what we should be in these structures, but we never truly know what it culminates to until we find ourselves playing the role in that specific structure.

We often measure ourselves against our own idea of what a good partner is; more often than not we give ourselves a good grade. This, I was guilty of. But then there was the Light, my mirror, who said not so fast. After grading myself an A, I asked for her feedback on my performance, and as I stood with the expectation of praise, I instead found myself more and more deflated as she expressed having feelings of loneliness and doubts about her decision to wed, as well as our future. The blow to my ego was near fatal, as for the year that passed, I thought I had done everything I was supposed to do. I worked multiple jobs to provide financially; no matter what weighted energy I was carrying, I always brought a smile to her; and I spent every free moment I had with her. I thought to myself: *What more could I possibly do?* Over the next years I would come to learn there were many answers to that question. While I was busy creating and maintaining a safe structure for our relationship, I was doing very little in giving myself to the Light. What she was requiring of me was a knowledge that I had never given to anyone. A knowledge of who I am, how I came to be, my deepest nightmares and fears, my scars, and my insecurities. I had shown her my laughter, but I hid my pain. She was always greeted with my smile but never experienced my tears. I shared all of my dreams but revealed nothing of what kept me up at night. I had convinced myself that I was doing this to protect her, but the truth is that I was hiding so much of me from her to protect myself.

Intimacy is a necessary binding agent for a relationship. In fact, there may not be a more essential ingredient that assists for growth and bonding. It is vital to the feminine as it is what fills her, and yet so few men understand what intimacy is. We so often confuse intimacy with passion, especially in love making. So many men know how to fuck their partner, but they have no idea how to fill her. This is because men are raised to be everything but intimate, and because throughout their dating life "loving" without intimacy is the mediocrity that they have been allowed to get away with.

Intimacy is vulnerability, and vulnerability to most men, is terrifying. It is terrifying because it is a nakedness. Not simply a physical nakedness, which many have no problem with, but a nakedness emotionally, mentally, and energetically. And it is not simply the act of being naked itself that brings about so much fear and anxiety, it is being naked in front of your partner, which comes with the risk of being rejected when she sees a part of you that has been deemed unfavorable or ugly by those who surround you, as well as by yourself.

One of the greatest steps that you can take on your journey to evolving into your highest self is to open yourself up to intimacy. In order to accomplish this, there are a number of measures that you must take. First, you must acknowledge that you have been injured in your past. It goes without saying that we live in a culture that constantly punishes us for exposing most of the emotional and energetic parts of ourselves, and this is a lesson learned very early on for most boys. Before they can comprehend language they are told "big boys do not cry," and around the age of seven, physical affection from a loving father becomes a thing of the past. It is time to become a man, and what that entails is being just about anything other than "soft," when softness is something that we all need to have access to within ourselves. Whenever a boy displays a tear, he is ridiculed, and we wonder why crying feels odd to men. It's easy to see these as trivial things, but over time, the bottling up of emotion becomes a toxic swell that explodes into some kind of violence. I can recall sitting in my car as a teenager, filled with so much pain, begging God to allow me to cry in order to get it out. I remember the feeling of my back pain leaving my body as I sobbed like a baby in the arms of the Healer, shedding the tears that I should have when I found out that I am an adoptee. When society, family, and friends take away a boy's right to express himself, they too take away a piece of his humanity, and an unfortunate reality is that in turn, he does the same to so many throughout his life. It is not only women that he robs with his lack of love and empathy, but his children, those who look up to him, and the men around him as well. To achieve intimacy, you must allow yourself the freedom to release the pain you are holding in, and heal.

Also, you should understand how your privilege is harming yourself as well as others, and by privilege I am referring to you being able to move from relationship to relationship without ever bearing yourself in front of a woman in ways other than physical. In all the other ways possible, we stand fully clothed while time and time again our feminine counterparts bare it all, or at least what we are willing to handle. This takes away from the potential, not only of what the relationship could be, but also what your partner could be as well as yourself. You may give just enough of yourself for the relationship to survive, but *just enough* will never be enough to grow. By opening yourself up, you subject yourself to the possibility of devastating pain, and at the same time you create space to evolve into higher levels of consciousness and love.

And so there I was, being everything that I thought a man and partner should be, all while fully clothed. I was clothed mentally, emotionally, spiritually, even energetically when what the Light really needed was for me to be naked, just as all women desire from their men. Her desire is beyond being taken care of by you, it is to be a part of you, it is to be whole with you.

The lesson itself reminds me of the story of Adam and Eve, and an often missed truth that resides in it. In this story, Adam and Eve were as close as two lovers could possibly be. They were of the same flesh and blood, they went about the business of fulfilling their purposes together, and they walked around completely naked without a single care in the world, until they acted in a way that brought about shame. It was in that moment, where this new feeling overwhelmed them, that they thought to cover themselves. While the story explains that they covered their bodies with leaves from a nearby tree, a deeper understanding reveals they were covering so much more. Before sin, Adam and Eve were naked in front of each other without a care in the world, just as two infants would be. They had no reason to hide a thing. However, when they were left with the scar of their sin, they felt the need to cover it, the same way we cover our own sins, shame, traumas, insecurities, and anything else that we feel may bring about rejection or ridicule. Adam and Eve, the closest of lovers, began hiding from another, which commenced their process of separation. What we hide from each other separates us, it is through revealing ourselves that we come closer, and to oneness again.

We are all participating in the dance of the masculine and feminine. Our desire to be with our polar opposite is also the eternal desire for oneness, just as the quest to achieve intimacy in relationships is the same as the energetic quest for oneness. The path to intimacy is rarely one walked with ease because of all the scars we accumulate along that journey, as well as the voices that warn us of ever displaying them. Because of this, we come just close enough for companionship and comfort, but when it comes to intimacy, the distance is as far as the eye can see.

A man must know the importance of closing the gap between safety and intimacy, and also accept that the closest thing he can find to real safety will be found in intimacy with someone who deeply cares for him. He must know that she needs to see his scars. She needs to know him. It is only when she has this knowledge that her healing feminine energy can move on his at its full potential. She has the ability to free herself and shower him with love, but that is only if he can be brave enough to allow it.

La petite mort

You need a woman who can destroy you. You may have been told that the way to your heart is through your stomach, and that a consistent supply of sex will keep you satisfied, but throughout the process of evolving, you will find that you need so much more as you, too, need intimacy. You need to explore your partner to know yourself. Just like the feminine, you feel the desire for closeness with your energetic opposite, and perhaps most importantly, you need a place to feel safe. Despite how much you may love your structures, they can still become a heavy load to hold, and despite how much you may be enjoying life, life can still place a lot on your shoulders. You need a place of rest. Nothing will bring you more peace than the embrace of a woman who you feel you can fully trust. In her care, you can take off your armor and let down your guard, you can express your emotions without fear of emasculation or ridicule; you can take off all the masks that you have to wear in the world. She is your home, a place where you can simply be. You need that slice of heaven on earth. Men often make the mistake of seeking this from the "other woman" whom he has no real ties to because he feels she cannot hurt him. They learn the hard way that everything they give in those vulnerable moments can be turned into the same bullets that take them down. Intimacy, for the masculine, can be found in the ability to surrender to the feminine. To find rest in something real. This is a part of the emptying that he needs.

Another emptying, of course, is that which is done through sex. You need to be with a woman who can destroy you, as this is what is necessary to be properly drained. The act of sex is just the process of creation on the opposing side of energy. She is draining you physically just as the feminine drains the masculine energetically, both are separate and the same, working through you time and time again to create. Whether or not you want a child, this is where the constant need to release is coming from, and you need a partner who can give you an orgasm that leaves you feeling decimated.

You need what the French call *la petite mort*, which is an orgasm likened to death. As morbid as that may sound, if you have experienced it, you know there is nothing better than being on the brink of losing consciousness after a climax. There is nothing other than this type of orgasm that will bring you closer to the kind of peace that metaphorically resembles death. This is an orgasm that makes you void of thoughts or energy, and leaves your body feeling blissfully weakened. You need this release. You know this because no matter how many times you pleasure yourself or have sex with energy that matches your own, you are never satisfied. It does not matter how skilled your sexual partner is if she does not have the energy you crave. You will look for the one who can give you this glorious "little death" as *la petite mort* is also often referred. Many will choose not to connect with the one who can offer this out of some fear or insecurity, but you may as well, because should she be available, you will find your way to her regardless. One of the worst feelings is to watch your structure crumble because you were too busy chasing the release the presumably safe woman you chose cannot give you.

In closing, love fearlessly.

A man is terribly afraid of loving a woman, but just the same, he is terribly attracted to her. This presents quite the conundrum. It often involves falling so deeply in love, offering so much promise, and then being a step away from committing to love, only to feel the heat of it and turn away. The heat that I am referring to is the impending suffering that will come with loving, which he can feel just as intensely as she can feel the possibilities of what could be should they decide to submit fully to love.

This is for the men who love to be loved by women, but are afraid of being vulnerable enough to love in return, and for the women who cannot understand why this keeps happening to them.

We should all understand and accept the fact that most men have an incredibly low level of emotional intelligence. This is a symptom, in large part, of the culture we live in, which tends to celebrate hyper-masculinity while frowning upon a man being in touch with the feminine. This is key, because the feminine is a part of self as much as yin is a part of the taijitu symbol. To deny the feminine is to deny self, and for this reason many men move throughout life without ever *being* whole. How can a man love the femininity of a woman if he cannot embrace the femininity of and within himself? Also, there is the issue of having the benefit of being able to be loved without the expectation of any meaningful level of vulnerability in return. In fact, the expectation is for men to be this way, to offer little more than what is on the surface, and so without an incentive to give more, they continue to deliver the bare minimum of their inner selves. Not only does this rob the relationship of intimacy, but it also robs both partners of exponential growth. To be vulnerable is to be naked, in any way, and what people are really afraid of when it comes to vulnerability is the rejection that may come of it when they are completely exposed.

Vulnerability is hard, but the reward is being made into better lovers of ourselves, and when we achieve that level of love, everyone benefits from our presence. Unfortunately, men are too often allowed to move through relationship after relationship without such exposure, and with each time it becomes harder for them to expose themselves.

By the time a man lets down his guard, opens up to his love, and truly extends his heart, it is because he *has* to. He tries the same act with the love of his life as he has with all of the others, only to fail, and in a last-ditch effort not to lose her, he attempts to do something he may have very little experience with, opening.

However he gets to that point, it truly is a magnificent piece of art to see. The always-still but now-exhausted masculine surrendering himself wholly into the healing bosom of the feminine, who herself, can barely stand under the weight of his pain but does so lovingly.

The fear of suffering is what holds many men from experiencing the fullness of love, and to those men, I must say, you will suffer anyway. Should you decide against loving entirely, you will suffer. Should you decide to love wholly, you will suffer. If you choose to protect yourself from the wild energy of the feminine, you will suffer. And if you surrender yourself into her arms, at some point, you will suffer. This is an odd thing to comprehend for many women, as I believe it is natural to think that an adult of a mature age should know and do better when it comes to key aspects of relating. For those who are confused, I will reiterate that this is the case for many men because they are not forced into a position wherein they have to challenge themselves emotionally, therefore they reap little rewards in terms of growth. Over and over again, women pour themselves into relationships while men give just enough to keep her there. Like clockwork, she feels the magnitude of heartbreak and despair, reaching higher levels of emotional maturity with each experience. This while men move from woman to woman, gaining experience on how to win her over, but hardly any on selflessness and intimacy. If you are ever puzzled as to how an adult male can be so clueless about love, understand that he never had to give it, and if he has once or twice experienced the pain of love, he may not want to again for quite some time. While women become accustomed to pain, men often avoid it, stunting them to the emotional intelligence of a teenager, if that.

To the man afraid of giving his all to love, I would say there is no need to fear love, nor the suffering that comes with it; in fact, it is entirely nonsensical to do so as it is inevitable. There is nothing more sought after than love. To love and to be loved is a blessing that you are here to experience in its fullness, both pain and joy. To rob yourself of that is to rob yourself of living.

In my opinion, there is love, and there is the absence of love. While peace can be found in the absence of love, for the most part, it is a terrible way to exist. Likewise, suffering can be found in love, but there is not a more delightful place to rest one's heart. This is why there is nothing more valuable and sought after than love. It is the first thing a newborn cries for, what we spend much of our lives in search of, and what we are terrified of living our last days without. Love is symphony and dance, ever-moving poetry, and any color of heaven that one can imagine. Love can also be devastating, as pain is a partner of love as the night is a partner of day. Few of us welcome that part of love or see the beauty in it. The part of love that forces one to see that it is elusive and stubborn, hell to catch, and impossible to control. Love causes us to give to the point of sacrifice, whether the gift is for another or ourselves. It fills hearts endlessly and breaks them without regard. Love is the God who gives and takes away. There is no escaping the joy or the pain of love, even those who choose to live without it must suffer with the void such a position leaves in their lives. There is no higher joy than what love delivers, and no greater an intensity of pain. Curiosity is the driving force of creation, but it is love that binds the masculine and feminine for a time so that creation can occur. This is why we cannot live without it. Love is the devil and the angel, a cause to our own heavens and hells, the greatest partner, the ultimate teacher, and a dangerous game for which we all must play.

The moment the Whole Woman placed her hand in the palm of mine is unforgettable. A small, yet terribly significant moment that I will hold dear to me forever. It was more than a touch. The fact that she was resting her hand in mine, how she did so affectionately, and everything that we felt in that moment was the point of all that we had experienced prior to that. It was the result of every single love gained and love lost, every setback, every tear as well as every moment of laughter. Every heartbreak, every disappointment, every longing, every hope, and every prayer. Every impactful memory whether forgotten or remembered. That one touch was the result of all of it. It was the end of the separate roads that led to the moment, and the birth of one we would walk together. It was deeper than love at first sight, it was knowing that we are for each other, and everything that ever was had to be in order for this to be.

What felt so good about this knowing was the feeling of completion. No longer would I have to take part in the dance of dating and moving in and out of relationships. The search was over. Two universes had collided to begin the process of merging into one. I had finally found my soulmate. And with that, came the overwhelming dread of it all. The fear of losing what felt so good to me, what I spent my entire life searching for. In the moment that she touched me, I also felt an agonizing pain of never feeling her touch again, as though it had already occurred in lives of the past.

To love, you must suffer, and this is what many are terrified of. They deny themselves the full spectrum of love because they are afraid of the pain that is involved. I knew in that moment that the end, however the end would come, would be devastating, but I also knew that loving and being loved by her would be worth the payment of devastating heartache. Try as we may, one cannot exist without the other.

Of course, there are many other ways to suffer when it comes to being in a loving relationship. To merge with another, there may have to be the death of parts of the individual. Even when that death is in the individual's best interest, it does not necessarily mean the process will be easy. There is suffering in sacrifice, forgiveness, growing, and selflessness. It is all necessary. What is not necessary is jealousy, possessiveness, power, and control, which only exist through a fear of losing love.

In the moment that the Whole Woman placed her hand into mine, I learned one of the most important lessons I ever have in regards to love, which is to feel the fear and do it anyway. Feel the fear of loss, feel all of your insecurities, feel everything that tells you not to do it because of the ways your heart has hurt in the past, and then love. You need no other reason than the fact that love is always worth it.

Next Steps

If you found this book valuable there are a couple of ways you can help me out. First off, it would really mean a lot to me if you could leave a rating and write a brief review on Amazon. Reviews are crucial to a book's success, and the more reviews this book receives, the more people will learn of self-love and evolving through the lessons I learned from wise women.

Secondly, you can also refer this book to a friend who you think would benefit from it, or share a link to the book on Facebook, Twitter, Pinterest, Reddit, etc. Word-of-mouth is still the best kind of advertising, and it would really help me out if you could tell others about what you learned in this book.

I welcome your comments and suggestions about this book at contact.jlford@gmail.com.

Thanks again for supporting my work.

About the Author

J.L.Ford Is an award winning writer, public speaker, and educator. His work on culture, relationships, self-help and spiritual growth has been enjoyed by millions of people all over the world.

You can follow J.L. on instagram @authorjl, and join him on Facebook at facebook.com/theauthorjl. www.whatshetaughtmebook.com.

Cover Art by Angela Lee inbox.angelalee@gmail.com
Editing by Christa Desir christa@christadesir.com

www.ingramcontent.com/pod-product-compliance
Lightning Source LLC
Chambersburg PA
CBHW070948180426
43194CB00041B/1713